CW00376857

FISHING FROM AFAR

The author at Coruisk (Skye)

FISHING FROM AFAR

by

STEPHEN JOHNSON

With illustrations from photographs

EXCELLENT PRESS
LUDLOW

First published in 1947
This edition published in 2006 by Excellent Press
9 Lower Raven Lane
Ludlow
Shropshire
SY8 1BW

A copy of the British Library Cataloguing in Publication Data for
this title is available from the British Library

ISBN 1 900318 24 5
Printed and bound in Great Britain

NEW FOREWORD BY BILL JOHNSON

I AM delighted that my father's book is being republished. It was written before I was born, and in circumstances I can barely imagine, in a world very different from the present day. But for me, father's personality shines through every paragraph—his humour, his endlessly inventive love of fishing, his natural keenness for country life and sport, and his kindness in wanting to share these things with others.

Dad was an excellent father to have. In his introduction, Tom Fort hints (rightly) that work wasn't exactly the top priority in father's life and I suppose his sons were among the chief beneficiaries of this arrangement. During school holidays there was always time to take us fishing on river or loch, and of course we had long weeks in Skye in the summer with all the freedom and adventure to grow up in. Nothing pleased him more than our fishing successes, and perhaps you would expect this of a father; but his generosity was wider than that, and there are many people who owe their introduction to fishing to his infectious enthusiasm and willingness to take the time to teach them.

Dad often said that he would get as much pleasure from rowing a boat on a loch or river and watching his companion catching a fish as catching it himself, and that was quite true—although it is also true that he had a strong tendency to grab the rod himself if the fish were taking particularly well.

For those of you who know my father only through this book, written when he was a young man, let me assure you that his love of fishing never diminished. He writes of flying low enough over rivers in the war to see if the trout were rising, and every time he drove over a bridge he looked for the same thing (complaining loudly if the wall was too high to see over). He was always looking for new methods to catch fish, and was enormously fond of dapping and its effectiveness in catching loch sea trout in daylight—and the hugely exciting rises it provokes. His love of Skye was the same at 85 (when he died there in 1997) as it was in childhood. The many long years of happiness that he must have longed for when he wrote this book in Stalag Luft III were truly realised.

Bill Johnson
Hennock, Devon, 2003

NEW INTRODUCTION BY TOM FORT

ON the 8th of December 1942 a British RAF officer, Stephen Johnson, took off from Marham in Norfolk, under orders to fly his Mosquito across the North Sea to Holland and drop four 500 pound bombs on the naval base at Den Helden. It was his first engagement with the enemy, and—as it turned out—his last. As he approached the target the plane came under tracer fire. Shortly after the bombs were dropped the port engine caught fire. Minutes later Johnson ditched in the Zuyder Zee. He and his observer managed to get into their dinghy. They were picked up by a Dutch fishing vessel and handed over to the Germans. Stephen Johnson spent the rest of the war as a prisoner.

It is, of course, idle to speculate what would have happened to him had he returned home from that first mission. He might well have been killed later; he might not. Had he survived the war, he might well have written an account of his fishing experiences, because he always had the literary impulse. And because he was, quite naturally, a writer, it would have been a good book.

But I think it is reasonably sure that it would not have been the same book as the one he did write, *Fishing From Afar*; and further, that it would have lacked something, for not having been written with pencil in a tatty dun-coloured notebook by a man with freezing feet and gnawing hunger, who never knew if he would see any of the precious places he was describing ever again.

To me, this is the rarest quality of an unusually fine fishing book: the astonishing vividness with which those precious places are depicted. That ability to capture, not merely the appearance of a river or lake, but the sound of it, the smell of it, the feel of it, must surely have been derived from Johnson's isolation. He did much more than just remember. He recreated a reality, to balance it against his current situation, to remind and convince himself that there was a better world where he belonged.

I know of no other fishing book which gives you, the reader, so strong a feeling of keeping the writer company. I felt this intensely the first time I read *Fishing From Afar*, many years ago. As a boy Johnson was taken each spring by his father from their home in Yorkshire across the Pennines to the Eden valley. They stayed in the little village of Edenhall, and fished the monarch and the princess among north-western trout rivers, the Eden and the Eamont. And I, as a boy, fished the very same water. I, too, did my apprenticeship fishing a team of three flies across and downstream. And I like to think the place means—and still means—as much to me as it did to him.

This is Johnson on a stretch familiar to me: "The Eamont at Udford is one of the loveliest stretches of water I know. It flows between red sandstone cliffs and wooded banks, with grass fields running down to the river in places. The river is a series of fast runs and pools, the water white and broken in places, but smooth enough in the pools to reflect the colours of the bank. The sound of water is always in the air, with the song of birds and call of woodpigeons superimposed". It was so then, in the 1920s, and it is so now; and I only have to read those sentences, and I am beside one of those pools, willing the olives to hatch and the swallows to dip and the trout to start to feed.

The same superb immediacy springs from his depiction of the place which was clearly closest to his heart, the Strathaird estate bought by his father after the First World War, which lies between Loch Slapin and Loch Scavaig in southern Skye, looking out towards the islands of Rhum and Eigg. At the tender age of four Johnson caught his first fish in the pool beside the house at Kilmarie, a brown trout of a pound, taken on a worm. But the

Stephen and his brother Mark, beside Stephen's Pool in the Kilmarie river.

cream of the fishing lay over the hill at Camasunary, in those days reached only by pony or after a long and often turbulent boat trip by sea. Into the bay flowed the river that took the sea-trout up to the lochs of na Creitach and an Athain. And around the next precipitous headland, in the shadow of the 3000 foot bulk of Garsbheinn, was the short stretch of river leading to Loch Coruisk—the "deep, dark, solitary lake", as Sir Walter Scott characterised it, squeezed into the heart of the soaring Cuillin Mountains.

The Johnson family—lucky devils!—spent their summers at Strathaird. "We lived a perfect life", Johnson recalled, "sleeping when we were tired and eating when we were hungry. We usually got up fairly late and had a large breakfast of porridge and sea trout. We spent the day fishing or stalking rabbits in the park with a rifle, with a snack for lunch. In the evening we had another meal of sea trout and raspberry tart or anything else that had been sent over the hill from Kilmarie".

And what fishing they had, in those blessed days! Johnson reckoned that on a good night on Loch na Creitach "one should catch from 10 to 15 fish weighing from 1 to 12 pounds". "But" he adds, "I have often had over 20". He and his brothers and their father caught sea trout in the sea, in the rivers, and on the lochs, by day and by night, all summer long. It is hardly surprising that Camasunary should have meant so much to him; nor that he should have become singularly adept at the varied arts of persuading these wonderful, unpredictable fish to take the fly.

But other places and other ways of fishing are brought to life in these pages: Bavaria in the 1930s, the Tweed in autumn, the Naver in spring, various English chalkstreams, a day after the big salmon of the diminutive Dorset Frome. But *Fishing From Afar* is very much more than a bran-tub of reminiscences of select rivers which the rest of us are very unlikely ever to get

Stephen fishing from a boat on Loch na Creitach circa 1973.

the chance to fish. It is packed with wisdom and common sense, all of it passed on in the most disarmingly unpretentious and accessible fashion. I also greatly admire Johnson for his philosophy of fishing.

For him the point of the exercise was to catch fish. "However much he (the fisherman) may like to hear the willow-warblers warbling in the willows, they are pretty poor compensation for a series of blank days' fishing", Johnson observed sanely and sagely. It is very evident that he wasn't particularly concerned with his equipment, as long as it did the job. Nor was he a tremendous scholar when it came to fly patterns. He focussed on the behaviour of fish—how to persuade them to take a fly or bait, how to get them into the net as quickly and efficiently as possible after they had done so. He fished unashamedly for the pot, was happy to eat trout or salmon almost every day of the week, and would—I suspect—have been outraged and astonished at any suggestion of returning them alive.

Although he exclusively pursued salmon and trout, and never seems to have concerned himself with the coarse species, he was entirely free of that accursed snobbery that is so often part of the mental baggage carried around by the game fisher. Here he is on the supposed moral superiority of fly fishing: "To me it is as thrilling to hook a fish on a minnow as on a salmon fly." He relished the chance to spin a golden or silver sprat on the Tweed, and did not look down his nose at the prawn. He stoutly defends the practice of fishing the wet fly downstream, asserting that it demands a high level of skill. For Johnson, fishing—though undoubtedly a consuming passion—was not a matter for academic study, nor for snootiness, nor (God forbid!) for solemnity. The idea was to catch fish and have fun.

Stephen Johnson was born in 1912, the middle of three brothers, all of them keen anglers. He was sent to Eton, and then spent a year in Germany, where—as he recorded in his privately published memoirs *A Kriegie's Log* ("Kriegie" was the slang for a POW)—he was supposed to learn the language sufficiently well to be able to read textbooks when he went up to Cambridge. "I did manage" Johnson says characteristically "to learn a smattering of German which I spoke with a marked Bavarian accent from drinking beer and going fishing with the natives".

The family expectation was that, after university, he would follow his father into the Middlesbrough engineering firm of Dorman Long. The prospect clearly appalled a young man used to the wide spaces and clean air of Skye. So he decided to become a vet, and spent five years engaged in not especially arduous study at the Royal Veterinary College in Camden Town, London. Hardly had he qualified than war broke out. Having learned to fly he became an instructor. Then came the fateful mission to Holland.

Johnson's account of his period in captivity is characteristic of the kind of man he was and the background he came from: full of laconic humour bordering on frivolity, very light on the business of being colder, more uncomfortable, more hungry and more bored than he could have believed possible; and on the strain that came from the constant, devouring uncertainty as to whether he would ever see home again. He never lost sight of his good fortune in being alive at all. "Hardly anybody ever got out of a Mosquito in difficulties", he wrote in *A Kriegie's Log*. "The next forty men from our squadron and 139 Squadron who were shot down were all killed".

He spent two years in Stalag Luft III, before being marched through the snows and numbing frost of the winter of 1944 to a camp south of Berlin, from where he was liberated by the Russians. Upon returning home, Johnson lived in Yorkshire for a time, where he met the woman who became his second wife, Brenda. The story of his wooing is quintessential Johnson. On the afternoon after meeting her for the first time at lunch, he took her to the River Ure at Masham to try out his new 13 foot salmon rod on a beat where no one had caught a salmon for years. The water was in flood, so he put on the biggest fly he had and—miraculously—hooked, played and landed a clean 17 pounder. "Her Yorkshire pudding is as light as ever, and she has many quick and excellent ways of cooking fish", is how his account ends.

Subsequently Johnson settled in Jedburgh, in the Scottish Borders, where both his brothers, Maurice and Mark, were farmers. He established a veterinary practice, but was careful—as his son, Bill, recalls—that it should never interfere with what he regarded as the priorities of life, fishing, shooting, and enjoyment. Their house stood on the banks of the Jed, a tributary of the Tweed and a first-rate place to teach his children and other youngsters how to cast a fly. Johnson took an especial delight in passing on his wisdom and experience; and is remembered as a gifted and highly entertaining teacher.

Jedwater House remained his home for the rest of a long and active life. But, fittingly, it was at his house in Strathaird that he died, in 1997. He and his brothers—who had jointly inherited Strathaird from their father—had disposed of much of the land in the 1970s, including the big house at Kilmarie. But they retained the part that was most important to them, Camasunary and the fishing on Coruisk and na Creitach. By the time of his death, Stephen Johnson had seen the end of the wonderful sea trout fishing that he enjoyed as a boy, and which lasted into the 1980s. Subsequently, with the development of the Scottish salmon farming industry, sea trout fishing collapsed throughout the Western Isles and along the west coast. As the cages multiplied, and ever more potent chemicals were used to keep the farmed fish free of the devouring sea lice, so did the populations of sea trout plummet.

To Alan Johnson, Stephen Johnson's nephew and the current owner of Camasunary, this downfall is nothing short of a tragedy, personal and ecological. Twenty years ago they were still averaging 600 fish a season, with a reasonable smattering of big fish of six pounds and above. Now the numbers are down to what Alan Johnson calls subsistence levels, and there are no big fish. The place retains its magical beauty. But without the sea trout, an irreplaceable element is missing.

Fishing From Afar was published in 1947. It does not appear to have made it to a second edition, so it seems reasonable to assume that sales were modest. In 1969 Johnson published *Fishing With A Purpose*, which mixes anecdote and sound

Stephen landing a fish in the Fisherman's Pool in the Camasunary river.

counsel in rather the same way as the earlier work, and has much of the same charm. This also failed to set the world alight. After that he was content to publish two further non-fishing volumes—*A Kriegie's Log* and *Mainly For Fun* (a collection of stories and light verses)—privately.

I have read and reread the two fishing books many times. I return to them because they capture in print the magic of the sport I love. They actually take you fishing, and that is something that can be said of very few of the 700 books on the subject under which my shelves groan. But, as is generally the case with magic, it is very difficult to analyse Johnson's secret. His style is clear and easy, his tone conversational, his manner self-deprecating. It is clear from the notebook in which he wrote *Fishing From Afar* that the distilling of experience into words came easily to him. The pencil flows smoothly, and there are remarkable few corrections. The revision, once he got home, was minimal—all he did was change the order of some of the chapters.

The overall effect is rather like finding a new friend. You meet, you shake hands, you find there is a common interest, you know you are going to get on. Reading Stephen Johnson is akin to listening to someone who knows their stuff and knows how to tell a story, is happy to listen as well as talk, whose conversation is full of laughter as well as wisdom and excitement. I should very much have liked to have known him and gone fishing with him. Reading this book is the next best thing.

Tom Fort
Reading, 2003

PREFACE

WHEN I was shot down in December 1942, I was put in a very small cell by myself and given far too little to eat, for eight long days. I couldn't even see out and I was allowed no books. There was absolutely nothing to do. All I had to amuse myself with was a brass button and two collar studs. The collar studs became goal posts and the button a ball. I was soon European champion at rolling that button between those posts.

I was terribly bored and I missed a great many things, but above all I longed for paper and pencil. I had always wanted to write about fishing and my memories were so vivid that I felt I must put them on paper.

When I was sent to Stalag Luft III, I managed to get a school notebook and pencil from the Education Officer, Tim Fenn. I spent an hour or two every day, miles away from that bleak, cheerless camp, recapturing my most pleasant memories. On several occasions I even forgot that my feet were freezing. As the year went round, I remembered all too clearly the things that I should have liked to be doing, and I wrote of them.

I found real pleasure in writing this book, and I hope people will enjoy reading it.

S.P.L.J.

CONTENTS

ILLUSTRATIONS

CHAPTER I

FOR BEGINNERS (WITHOUT TEARS)

THE charm and fascination of fishing lies in its enormous variation and the delightful places where one goes to fish. From the sleepy warmth of a Hampshire chalk stream on a June evening to the bitter cold of a Scottish salmon river in Spring, with the ice freezing on the rings of the rod and snowstorms sweeping across the bleak brown moors, but always the chance of the exquisite thrill of catching a spring salmon. Every river and loch has its own charm, and when fishing, one constantly finds or rediscovers scenes that make an indelible impression, which one can remember through long dreary months.

The popular misconception of a fly fisherman seems to be of a lazy man with a great deal more patience and imagination than he has regard for the truth. The public forms its opinion of the patience required from the rows of men who go coarse fishing on a Sunday, and frequently sit in the same place all day and never catch anything but a cold in the head. For the fly fisherman too much patience is definitely a disadvantage, as the chances are that on a particular day fish will take a certain fly presented in only one way and won't look at anything else. This applies especially to salmon and sea trout. The patient man who goes on slogging away all day fishing a sunken fly downstream for salmon may have nothing but his perseverance with which to console himself in the evening; whereas the impatient man who only fishes the same way for half an hour unless he gets results and then tries another fly or fishing with a greased line, may strike the presentation that tickles the fancy of the fickle fish, and go home with a fat salmon. Although the feeling of self-righteousness is quite sustaining, I should rather have a salmon.

It is rather unfair that fishermen are always branded as liars, but as a result of this supposed characteristic most fishermen are scrupulously accurate in all they say, or even tend to understatements. The trouble is that in any other form of sport the size of the quarry can't vary greatly although one hears of 'the biggest fox that was ever seen!' When one is ferreting rabbits the biggest thing that can appear is a full-sized rabbit, but fishing a great deep loch one may hook a fish of any size. This aspect of fishing appealed to me very strongly at an early age, but I admit it is awfully easy to exaggerate the size of a fish that gets off to oneself anyway. The pity of having such a reputation is that one doesn't like to tell of unlikely things that really do happen.

I remember telling a friend of something that happened when I was fishing the Wiltshire Avon with him, and he said 'I believe you, but don't tell anybody else', and it was quite a likely story. If one catches the branch of a tree or a telegraph wire, what generally happens is that the cast goes round the obstacle and the fly gets hooked on to the cast again, so the more one pulls the tighter this form of slip-knot becomes. I was fishing the big shallow below the mill at Durnford. There was a tremendous hatch of fly with hundreds of swallows flying up and down the river. Suddenly my cast caught behind me, where I knew there was no tree. I found that the cast had become caught round a swallow's wing in the way I mentioned above and it came down out of control. The bird was none the worse but chattered indignantly when I unhooked the cast, and flew away quite happily when it was released. Quite a simple little story, but if told by a fisherman there wasn't a chance of it being believed.

When you begin fishing you will be branded as a harmless liar at once, but you won't need much patience unless it is with the people who will say to you: 'I could never be a fisherman, it needs too much patience.' I assure you that you will soon feel a strong desire to clock these people on the head, as every non-fisherman will say it to you when he starts talking about fishing out of politeness, and he will give a kind of complacent simper as he says it . . . .

There are many shops where the inventions of man for luring fish from their natural element are for sale. The man behind the counter dreams of the day when someone will walk in and say: 'I am just taking up fishing. I wish to be fully equipped for fishing salmon, sea trout and brown trout anywhere in the British Isles, money is no object.' The manager would be sent for and they would start off by selling their victim at least ten rods averaging £15 in price, with reels to match costing £5 each before they began on the casts and traces, lines and flies. The salmon flies alone would number several hundreds at 2s 6d apiece.

It is a great error ever to admit ignorance when entering a shop. I once made the mistake of going into a famous London tackle shop and saying that I knew nothing about fishing for hüchen and would they please tell me? We were going to Seefeld in Austria for a skiing holiday one Christmas and Seefeld is near Innsbruck, which is on the Inn, out of which I hoped to catch a hüchen—an enormous fish that lives in the Danube and runs up its tributaries to spawn. They consulted great books on hüchen fishing and said that I should have to have special tackles made for mounting the baits, with the flanges to make it spin set well back and the triangles at the head, as the hüchen always seizes its prey by the head. I could only say meekly 'Oh, ah yes!' and pay the enormous bill when it arrived. I never did catch a hüchen or even fish for one. When we arrived at Innsbruck the rest of the party went straight to Seefeld, while I visited the local tackle shop and discovered that hüchen didn't come up as far as Innsbruck at that time of year, but the beauty of that afternoon made up for the disappointment. It was Christmas eve and there was a Christmas-tree market in one of the squares surrounded by old houses with paintings on the whitewashed walls. Men women and children, warmly dressed, came and went carrying their little trees. High above the town rose the snow-covered peaks of the Wetterstein mountains, and as the sun sank it left the valley in shadow and shone redly on the high mountain tops.

I managed to get my own back on the London tackle shop the following summer. There is a fish that lives in the Wiske, which runs into the Swale in Yorkshire, called a burbot. It is dark in colour and shaped rather like an eel. It was originally brought from Italy and put into the fish-ponds at Mount Grace Priory by the monks who wanted to be sure of their Friday dinners. When Henry VIII had trouble with his wives and took it out on the monks by knocking down their monasteries, the fish-ponds went into disrepair and the burbots escaped into the Wiske, where they have lived ever since. When my father and an uncle were boys they caught these fish by putting drain-pipes into the river in likely-looking places and leaving them for a few days. The fish were caught by putting a hand at each end of the pipe, lifting it out of the water and saying 'Are you there?' One day a cousin and I were feeling very facetious and we walked into the shop, trying hard not to laugh, and asked for half a dozen burbot tackle. The man gulped a bit and said 'Yes, sir.' We left the next move to him, and eventually he said: 'Pardon me, sir, but wouldn't it be worm tackle that you are needing?' and we had the satisfaction of telling him how burbots were caught.

There are many pitfalls for the unwary beginner. Fishing tackle looks so attractive in a shop, that even veterans buy many worthless gadgets and lures, so how is the beginner to avoid buying things that he will never need? As a rule one starts fishing with enough tackle to fill a bag, and the longer one fishes the more one discards until everything one needs will fit into one pocket. Much the best plan is to find someone who is a fisherman to help one start buying fishing tackle.

If the beginner is going to start to fish for salmon he must have salmon tackle, but most people start with trout. The first consideration is a rod which will serve to catch fish under as many different conditions as possible and is easy to cast with. I should advise a 9 feet 6 inches split cane, as on it one can catch anything from a trout with a dry fly to a small salmon in low water. Rods all look alike when they are produced in a shop, but a man who has done some fishing is invaluable in helping to select one, as they all differ in action. With some rods anyone can throw a good line, while with others it is quite impossible although they are just as expensive and highly varnished. It is possible to buy a good rod 9 feet 6 inches for £5, but in London it will cost nearer £10.

It is a mistake to economise in buying a reel, and a good reel is an investment that will never be regretted. It should balance the rod—a fisherman will be able to feel this—and it should be large enough in the drum to take 40 yards of double-tapered casting line and 60 yards of undressed silk backing. The finest cast used is 4x and the strongest trout size is 1x. A tapered cast is a definite help when casting into a wind, besides being economical. If a break occurs it will be at the weakest point and only the last piece of cast or point, as it is called, will be lost. Most casts are made of silkworm gut and even in war-time they could be obtained although the gut is imported from Spain. It is primarily used for surgery and the pieces which are no good for this are used for making casts. There are several substitutes for silkworm gut but I have never found anything as good, although some good alternative will probably be found some day.

All we want now, before we start fishing, is the actual flies. Trout flies are, on the whole, imitations or near imitations of natural insects, although there are many different interpretations of each natural insect which fish have been observed to take. It is always worth while remembering that the fish doesn't pay the bill. Flies, especially salmon flies, which aren't the imitation of any living animal, are tied to sell rather than to catch fish. On the whole shop-tied salmon flies are overdressed and far too tidy-looking. They are works of art and look beautiful when arranged in a shiny tin; but when they become chewed about, lose half their feathers and look rather scruffy, they are far more likely to catch fish.

It is well worth while starting to tie one's own flies soon after beginning to fish. It is quite easy to tie flies which will catch fish and I catch most of my fish on flies I have tied myself although I am sure nobody would buy one if he saw it in a tackle shop. When I first started making my own flies a ghillie in Skye said: 'Ach, Master Stephen will never have to buy any more flies!' but actually it is very little cheaper making one's own than buying shop-tied flies. The advantage is that one can tie flies just the way one wants them and try out new patterns on the unsuspecting fish. I have discovered two original flies which under certain conditions will catch sea trout better than any other, entirely by experimenting over a number of years. It is difficult to have complete confidence in the rather scruffy-looking flies that one ties when one starts, but after persevering and catching a few fish this is soon acquired.

On the whole it is best to buy flies from a shop near where one is going to fish. It is most exasperating, after procuring a box full of expensive salmon flies for a ghillie to select from, if he says, 'Ach, they're no good', and takes a dirty great hairy creature from his own cap and ties it on. Your flies are almost certainly as good as his, but if he has no confidence in the fly you are fishing with, you will soon find yourself doubting it also. Lack of confidence is very infectious.

It is convenient to have a tin in which to keep flies and casts and these make admirable Christmas and birthday presents, but resist the temptation to buy more than is absolutely necessary. With a little ingenuity a 'flat 50' cigarette tin makes an excellent fly or cast box.

Rod, reel, line, cast, fly, are all bought and assembled: the problem now is how to catch the fish. I have taught many people to fish and of one thing I am quite convinced: the sooner they catch a fish, however small, the more likely they are to become keen fishermen and not say: 'Well, if that's fishing, I don't like it.' There is no thrill like hooking and playing a fish and it will make people keen when nothing else will.

It is a good plan to start fishing on a lawn in order to get the feel of the casting. My father used to describe the actual motion as being similar to throwing an empty cartridge off a stick. Be firm with the rod, but don't force it, and remember the line must have time to go straight out behind before it is brought forward again. Once one can cast a reasonable line of about 8 yards one out of three times, it is time to think of trying on water, for however expertly one casts on a lawn there is very little chance of catching a fish. One of my nightmares is that I am fishing and I suddenly find I am in a room and realise that the only way that a fish can get at a fly is by coming in through the door.

Above Camasunary (Skye)

Even if one fishes pretty badly in water, there is just a chance of catching a fish, and it is that hope and chance which keeps the beginner's interest from waning.

I always select a place which is as easily fished as possible for starting operations. The ideal is a pool in a river with a good flow in the centre and slack water under the near bank. There should be a gentle wind down and across the stream and no trees or bushes within reach. The pool should also hold fish.

The seapool at Camasunary answers all these requirements and I took a young friend there one day. There was quite a good water in the river and I assured her that she couldn't fail to catch a fish, although I was far from feeling as confident as I appeared. The wind was just right and floated the fly out across the river. She made about one good cast in three, but when they weren't so good the stream soon straightened the line and the fly worked round from the quick to the slowly moving water very nicely. I kept a watchful eye on the fly while she was casting to make sure it didn't touch the stones behind, as that will generally knock the point or the barb off the hook. I was terribly excited when she hooked one, and crouched at the edge of the shingle with the net, and hoped it wouldn't get off. She caught three sea trout without any help from me and I have never been more delighted about any three fish.

The next easiest place to fish is on a loch from a boat, if there is a gentle breeze. There is an artificial loch near Kilmarie house and I have often taken people there who were just learning to fish. There is just enough peat stain in the water to make a long line unnecessary and the sea trout sometimes take very well in the evening between tea and dinner. The difference between hooking a fish in moving and in still water, is that when a fish takes in still water the fisherman must strike. When one is ghillieing a novice, one has to watch for a rise all the time and shout 'strike!' as soon as a fish rises, as the novice generally has very little idea of where the fly is, and what a rise looks like.

I have the greatest respect for anyone who starts fishing on a dry-fly stream and perseveres until he catches a fish, as a high degree of skill is necessary before one can nearly catch a trout from a chalk stream. Brown trout can be fairly easy to catch, but on the whole I think sea trout should be the object of the novice's attention. If he can find a pool in a river in August that hasn't been visited for a few days and if there is a spate, there is a good chance of encountering a young and immature sea trout of ¾ lb that knows as little about fishing as he does. Then there is a good sporting chance that it will take and be hooked.

CHAPTER II

THE STRIKE

By the word 'striking' I mean 'the action performed by the fisherman which if properly executed results in the fish being hooked.' It may describe an arc through the air and end up in the heather about 10 yards away to be pounced upon by a small boy, or remain in its natural element with an iron blue dun skilfully embedded in the corner of its mouth, to be tired by an even more tired business man. Salmon fishermen don't like the word 'strike' in this connection, as in many cases the weight of the water on the line draws the hook home into the fish's mouth; or the fish does this itself by turning against a light line. But in trout fishing there is usually some action on the fisherman's part which hooks the fish.

The most difficult method of fishing from the striking point of view is downstream wet-fly fishing. This is the easiest way of fishing for casting. The fish sees the fly coming towards him and allows for it approaching at the same speed as other insects carried by the stream, whereas it is actually being pulled against the current, and the fish often misses the fly altogether. If the water is very broken and the fly well sunk no sign of the rise will be seen, and if he does touch it the result is generally a pull and nothing else. The proportion of pricked fish to hooked fish is generally very high, something like 3 to 1. This is a strong argument against downstream wet-fly fishing. I have found that the chances of hooking a fish depend largely on the length of line being used. It is far easier to hook a fish downstream on a fairly short line. If a long line is used to reach a likely spot, a fish may be risen but it is very seldom hooked. Most important of all is the human factor. One day hardly a fish is missed and they are all firmly hooked, while the next it is impossible to hook a thing, and the ones that are hooked get off after a few kicks. The same thing happens in dry-fly fishing but I don't think one should blame the fish for coming short every time.

For the beginner there is a great tendency to strike too hard. I remember my first day's fishing on the Eamont in Westmorland. I was eleven at the time and using a 3x cast after being accustomed to a 1x cast for sea trout. I threw quite a good enough line to rise the fish, but whenever I felt a pull I struck far too hard and if the fish had taken the fly properly I left it embedded in its jaw. I think I lost about ten flies that day and never hooked a fish. I can still remember how my legs ached on the way home in the car after walking in waders all day.

My brother suffered from the same trouble when he started, and on two occasions he struck with such vigour that he lost a dropper in the fish's mouth and foul-hooked it with the tail fly. Each time he landed the fish and recovered the dropper, but I hate to think how many flies he must have lost as the odds against doing this must be terrific. He had even greater difficulty than I in stopping himself from striking too hard, and I believe he still strikes off the reel with the check set very light, although it is possible to strike a fly off even under these conditions if done with sufficient quickness and strength. When the rod is raised the first movement of the point is down, and then quickly up again. It is easier to strike gently if the rod point is kept fairly high above the water, whereas it is almost impossible if the point is kept too low. My advice, if you find you are striking too hard, is to lessen the check of the reel and allow the line to run uninterrupted from the reel to the first ring all the time the fly is fishing, although it is necessary to put a finger over it before casting. Also, remember to keep the rod point well up when the fly is in the water. The stronger the current the higher the point of the rod should be kept, as in fast water the fish will come with more of a bang than in slow water.

My own trouble often is that, without striking the fly off in the fish, I still strike too hard to hook the fish on a No. 0 or No. 1 hook. I used to think this was impossible using a 3x or a 4x point, but I am sure I often do it both wet-fly and dry-fly fishing. One day I actually proved it to myself. I was fishing a

The Eamont (Westmorland)

fast run on the Eamont and rose five fish in quick succession. Each one I struck rather too hard and I either felt them fairly heavily or actually had them on for a second or two before they got off. I got rather cross at missing so many opportunities so I began fishing with my left hand, with which I am much more gentle, and the next three fish which rose I hooked and landed.

I usually prefer a floating line for wet-fly fishing, as it keeps the line straighter and the fly nearer the surface and one is more likely to see a rise. One can be quicker on the strike, and so one can afford to use a slightly longer line if there is a likely place rather far out. The disadvantage of a greased line is when the cast insists on floating and the flies skim along the surface leaving a wake like a flotilla of destroyers. This is maddening as it often happens on a smooth glide, for fish will never take.

It is much easier to hook a fish wet-fly when fishing upstream with a fairly short line, because one can afford to use a shorter line than fishing downstream as the fish are looking away from one. The flies sink more quickly, and unless a fish rises within the first few seconds of their landing on the water it is unlikely that the rise will be seen. The usual signal that something has happened is the line stopping coming towards one. I always try to watch the knot between the line and the cast, and as soon as it stops I raise the rod point. If I actually see it stop, I generally hook the fish, but if I am looking away and look back to find it has stopped, I am usually too late and just feel the fish for a second. Fishing upstream with a short line one should seldom miss a fish; also they are usually better hooked than those hooked fishing downstream, as the fly is being pulled into their mouths, and not out when one strikes. The flies are floating naturally in the current, so the fish is less likely to miss them.

I remember the first time I tried fishing upstream I was quite a small boy. There is a lovely pool on the Eamont just above Udford ford. The head of the pool is fairly broad and there is a lot of green weed on the bottom. The water is fast, without being broken, and fairly shallow. There was quite a strong upstream breeze blowing which had been bothering me all morning. I sat watching the pool as I had lunch, and after a few minutes I saw some fish beginning to rise at the head, so I went to investigate. There was a good hatch of olives being blown up the pool, but when they reached the faster water at the head of the pool the current drifted them down again as fast as they were being blown up, so there was a great concentration of flies. I waded out below where the fish were rising, within about an inch of the top of my waders, and began fishing. The water seemed full of fish taking the floating flies as fast as they could, but they took a sunk waterhen bloa equally well. As soon as I hooked a fish he bolted downstream either past me or through my legs, and I was properly tied up once or twice with my landing-net and rod. I also made the mistake of leaning forward to land the fish, so the water poured into the back of my waders. I remember I couldn't think where it was coming from, but I was much too excited to worry about little things like wet feet! When a fish was hooked he didn't disturb the rest of the rising fish and I managed to catch eight from practically the same position in about half an hour. They were all over 12 inches and in very good condition. At the time it was my best basket of fish so I was an upstream enthusiast from that moment on. I still think it is best to fish upstream if fish can be seen rising to the natural fly, but otherwise on broad fast water I prefer to fish downstream and across, 'mending the line' to make the fly move through the water at as even a speed as possible.

In dry-fly fishing striking is much more of an exact art than in wet-fly fishing, for as a rule one can see the fish take the fly and so time the strike as one thinks best. Here again on some days I find I hook practically every fish I rise, while on others I never hook a single fish. On the 'bad' days I can never make up my mind whether it is entirely my fault or whether the fish aren't taking properly. I like to think it is sometimes the fish's fault, but if I feel the fish at all I think it is entirely my own fault that I don't hook it. Sometimes the explanation of missing a fish is that the fly has dragged at the last second. There is a moment after the fish has opened his mouth to take a fly and before he has closed it again when it is out of his sight. If a drag comes on then it will be enough to make him miss the fly, but it won't put him down in the same way that seeing the fly drag would do. If the water is fairly fast and rough he may rise again just as freely the next time the fly comes over him, but if he misses it several times he will become suspicious. This shows that a fish in fast water must quite often miss a natural fly. I wonder if flies ever see a fish's mouth coming towards them through the water and take avoiding action, although there can't be much future in turning in towards that attack!

There is one certain way of missing a fish and that is by striking when a spectator says 'You've got him'. People have invented various rules for judging a strike. One is saying, 'One thousand, two thousand' after the fish has risen before raising the rod point. This is quite a good standby for an ordinary length of line and a normal fish, but the shorter the line the more time must be given before striking. Many a time on a very short line I have seen the fish's mouth actually close on the fly before striking and still been too early. This is especially easy if the fish is under an overhanging bush and the rod point has been pushed through it with the fly wound in to within a foot or so of the tip of the rod and dropped on the fish's nose. I have never tried leaving the fly entirely alone to see how long it is before the fish spits it out again, as I have always wanted to catch the fish, but I must try it if I can escape from this place and get to a river. I believe it will be a much longer time than one expects. With a long line one should strike as soon as the fish is seen to rise and take the fly, as there is bound to be some slack line and it takes some time for the strike to be communicated to the hook.

I believe another important consideration is the size of the fish. The larger the fish the slower one should strike. Is this merely that one is more excited with a big fish or do they really take a fly more slowly? I think they really do take more slowly, apart from the fact that they have bigger mouths and it must take the fly longer to reach the back of them. A little fish is seldom certain of his position and is in a hurry to get his food in case he is turned out, while a big 'un can afford to suck in flies at his leisure without fear of interruption to his meal;

besides, a fly is such a tiny morsel that if a big fish spends much energy on taking one he must be losing on the deal, and that is no way for trout to put on weight.

I always find it much easier to strike fish in fast water than in slow water. In fast water the fish has to make up his mind and move much more quickly so one can afford to strike sooner. In sluggish water everything seems to happen in slow motion. The fish comes lazily up to take a good look at the fly and one can almost see him make up his mind; then he slowly opens and shuts his mouth on the fly. My conclusion is that with a large fish in slow water on a short line it is impossible to strike too slowly and almost impossible to strike slowly enough. With a small fish in fast water and with a long line one can strike as quickly as one likes, but one has no business to be fishing for him anyway. I am sure more fish are missed by being too quick than too slow when the fisherman can see exactly what is happening all the time. I am probably being too honest in admitting the number of fish I miss on chalk streams, for I seldom read an account of a day's dry-fly fishing on which the author has missed any. Some people even claim they can put the fly where they like in the fish's mouth; but this is rather like the 'captain' who always shot his birds in the eye.

When fishing a nymph upstream on a chalk stream, and if the fish follows the nymph at all, the correct time to strike is when the fish has turned back to its original position. This is usually easier than it sounds, as one can seldom see the fish take the nymph unless the light is very good, although one knows that the fish took something fairly near where one's nymph must have been. I am always pleasantly surprised when I strike and find the fish on the other end. A fish often follows a nymph several yards, and I wonder if it waits until it gets home again before it eats it. I rather think it must or it would probably find something wrong with the hardness of a weighted hook which even the purest of purists use when nobody is looking.

It is extraordinary that one can sometimes strike and feel a fish quite hard without putting it down. I remember a fish this summer on the Anton which I rose and definitely felt fairly hard. He sank down slightly discouraged, but within a few minutes he was taking the natural fly again. I tried him with another fly, as the sight of the same fly will generally put a fish down for good. After inspecting it several times he eventually took and I managed to land him.

My striking was most inaccurate on the days I managed to get this summer. My mother always says that if she is playing a large sea trout and begins thinking how well it will do cold for lunch on Sunday it invariably gets off. Perhaps it was this aspect of fishing that made my striking so bad, as a brace of fat trout are a great asset to the larder in a small household. I did have one triumph however. I had caught one trout, but there were very few rising and we decided to go home to dinner. I had already taken my rod down when we saw a fish rising quite regularly. The chances against my hooking it were pretty big judging by the form I had been showing lately, but I put up the rod again and caught the fish and very good it was for breakfast.

It is comparatively easy to give some idea of when to strike a brown trout, but not with sea trout, as they take in so many different ways that it is very difficult to give any advice on when to strike. I have quite often seen sea trout come up to a floating fly and make a perfect head-and-tail rise, but omit the important point of opening their mouths, and they sometimes make a splashy rise trying to drown the fly. There are many different ways that sea trout in a loch may approach and take a fly, but they seem to have an understanding among themselves, and generally all behave in the same way on the same day. I had one good day on Loch na Creitach in Skye when I caught eight fish weighing 17 lbs. The biggest was 3½ lbs and the smallest 1½ lbs and I hardly rose another fish besides the ones I caught. They all took with a good swirl and a hard pull and six out of the eight were hooked in the corner of the mouth. On another day I caught a slightly smaller basket of the same-sized fish, but not one of them broke the surface and they took so gently that I only felt the faintest draw on the line. Once two of us were fishing and we each caught a fish of about 2½ lbs. Both were hooked in the dorsal fin. They were the only rises either of us had one drift.

For loch fishing, when the fly is being worked towards the boat fairly slowly, it is usually best to strike as soon as a rise is seen or a pull is felt. Since the rise is generally made by the fish turning away after it has taken the fly, this will not be too soon, and the chances are that if the fish has taken properly it will be well hooked. If the fish breaks the water to take a floating fly, or one very near the surface, one must wait until it disappears before striking. Sea trout rising to a floating fly quite often make a head-and-tail rise and it is very easy to strike when the head appears, which is much too quick. It is essential to wait until the tail is seen and preferably until it disappears, although it feels an awfully long time if the fish is a big one.

Another occasion when sea trout break the water to take is when one is fishing with an artificial sand eel in the sea. The first time we tried one of these was in Camasunary Bay. There was a strong south wind blowing and the waves were fairly big, but we saw a number of fish jumping about 100 yards out opposite the mouth of a burn where they often seem to congregate, so we went for the boat. It was hard work rowing into the wind and across the swell but eventually we were opposite the place where we had seen the fish. I kept rowing with the bows into the wind while A. knelt in the stern and fished downwind. The fish were in about 8 ft of water, and sometimes there wouldn't be a fish to be seen while a few minutes later some would jump and others just break the waves. They kept fairly close together and within a hundred yards of the same place. A. began fishing with a small salmon fly, but although he cast right among the fish they took little notice. Occasionally one would follow the fly and swirl at it; one or two took a hold, but he only landed one. He then produced an artificial sand eel made of sole's skin painted blue and silver, about 1 inch long. 'The man in the shop' had assured him that it was the thing to catch sea trout in tidal water, and A. like myself will always try anything once. Although it didn't look a very likely lure, this seemed the moment to try it. We changed places and I started fishing while A. tried to row the boat. I believe he is a good cricketer. The effect on the fish was terrific; as soon as the lure landed on the water a fish of about 2 lbs flung itself out of a wave towards it, but I was too quick for it and snatched the lure away before it got there. I thought the fish might have taken coming up and knew that quick striking is usually the order of the day when fishing in the sea. That fish definitely had a puzzled look on its face just before it landed where its tea should have been. The next cast another fish flung itself out of the water; but this time I waited until it descended again before I struck, and I hooked him. The conditions were fairly bad for playing and landing a fish as the boat was rising and falling on a big steep swell, and sea trout in the sea are tremendously lively, but we eventually landed him, a fish of 2½ lbs. We went on fishing and whenever the fish was near the surface and showing, if the sand eel landed near them, one would have a go at it. There were some big fish about but the biggest one A. landed was 3½ lbs although I believe he lost one of over 6 lbs. When a lot were showing we tried to cast over the biggest, but a little one generally took before the big one could get to it. We caught six in about an hour, before the tide went out and the fish became discouraged and moved away. It was a most amusing afternoon. All the fish we rose on the sand eel behaved in exactly the same way. They jumped sideways out of the water, as a salmon jumps, and seized the sand eel as they landed back in the water. This must be the way they take the natural sand eel when they are near the surface.

As a rule when fishing in the sea or tidal water a great number of fish follow the fly for every one that takes. When they do take they make a snatch at it and then spit it out again. They may only have it in their mouths for a second, and quite often after missing a number, one hooks a fish just as one is taking the fly out for a new cast, and so anticipating the rise. They do occasionally take a firm hold, but the majority of times they take very short, and a long line or a bow in the line, from fishing across or into a wind, will make striking very difficult. In all these cases the quicker one can strike the better the chance of hooking the fish.

Sea trout in a river usually take in much the same way as in tidal waters, although they are not so inclined to come short. If there is a spate and a new run of fish come into the river they very often take a good hold, but the following day they often take very short.

At night they take in an entirely different manner, whether they are in tidal water, or a loch. They just seem to arrest the fly's progress and unless one strikes the moment a check is felt it is too late. If one is not working the fly fairly fast through the water the check may not be felt until the fish has spat the fly out again. A great many fish are missed by striking too slowly at night, but when one does strike right and there is a large fish at the other end, it feels exactly like striking a log for a moment and then the fun begins. If it is in tidal water the fish will probably be in the air as much as in the water, and if it is too dark to see what he is doing the chances are he will escape. A fresh sea trout's mouth is a very soft and delicate thing and the jar of its falling back into the water against a tight line will often break the hold.

I have fished for sea trout since my Nanny put the worm on the hook and played the fish while I just held the rod and shouted for her when anything happened. I have the quick strike in my veins, so I probably miss more trout than most people, and hook quite a lot of sea trout.

The golden rule for striking salmon is 'don't'. With a sunk fly and line the temptation to strike isn't quite as great as with a greased line. If the rod point is kept low and a finger on the line the fish will hook itself by turning against the tight line, and when a steady pull is felt all that is needed is to raise the rod point slowly. With a greased line most people like to have a few feet of loose line between the reel and the first ring: When a fish takes they let this line go. An alternative is to have the check of the reel set very light and allow it to turn a couple of times before raising the rod point. It is difficult to stop oneself striking, especially when the fish takes with a head-and-tail rise, but I can usually manage it and watch the line stealing away across the water without any violent reaction. They say it is fatal to strike at once and I believe it is, but when the fish spits the fly out again before he is hooked, I sometimes wonder whether a good quick strike mightn't have done the trick and hooked me a salmon. This happened on the last day's salmon fishing I had before I was *abgeschossen* and the Germans who pulled me out of the Zuider Zee said, 'The war for you is ended, yes?' I was fishing the long stream on the Rutherford beat of Tweed in the autumn. The river was fairly low so I was using a greased line and small fly. I can still see the line begin to move away across the water as I let him have the slack line I was holding, but before he took it all up he let go. If I had struck should I have had him? I have plenty of time to think it over anyway.

CHAPTER III

ABOUT PLAYING FISH

I WAS fishing the Loisach in Bavaria, spinning with an artificial minnow, when a fish took just as the bait was coming into the fast shallow water at the edge of the pool. He must have followed the bait from the deep pool as he took in about 18 inches of water. I struck fairly hard as soon as I felt him and he was so flustered that he ran straight towards the shore. I encouraged him by running backwards and within a few seconds of taking he was on the shingle, a fat rainbow trout of about 1½ lbs, kicking like mad and wondering what had happened. I managed to reach him before he could get back into the water again and he was in the bag or rather the wooden water-container in which he had to be transported back to the hotel to which the fishing belonged. Peter, who was watching the performance, was thoroughly shocked and said 'But you haven't played him yet' in tones of horror.

Playing a fish is usually a necessary interlude between hooking a fish and landing it. Although it is probably the most exciting part of fishing, it is carried out with just one end in view, that is, to land the fish, and it wants to be kept as short as possible. There is a great difference between playing a fish and playing with a fish. One should have every possible advantage of rod and tackle before starting the job, and it is a mistake to use too light tackle. The strength of the tackle, especially the cast, should depend on how much the fish is prepared to ignore. This is learnt by experience, one's own or somebody else's. If a trout will take a fly on a 2x cast, there is no point in using a cast as fine as 4x if one wants to catch as many fish as possible, which is generally the reason for going fishing. The use of too light tackle will mean a number of fish breaking the cast and escaping with a fly in their mouths.

The greatest range of strength in tackle is in salmon fishing.

Salmon are landed on anything from piano wire which would lift a man, to trout casts which would break with a few pounds' strain, and a very few are landed on twisted wire traces, those inventions of the devil. There has been a strong tendency recently to fish with smaller rods and lighter tackle. Now thread-line reels and microscopic spinning rods are used and people boast of the size of fish compared with the size of rod, but surely the answer is why not use a proper-sized rod? It might be excusable if the fisherman were weak and undersized, but to see a great man about 6 ft 6 in. tall and broad in proportion using a 4-ft spinning rod always makes me laugh. Thread-line fishing is still very popular on some rivers, but on others where the fish run big it is banned. It has its advantages and disadvantages which are quickly found out. Personally, I don't like it and for fishing very light I had much prefer a multiplying reel, and a rod about 8 ft, although my brother rudely alludes to my reel as 'that wrist watch'.

The function of the rod in playing a fish is to ensure an even strain on the cast, which is usually the weakest link in one's connection with the fish. When the fish kicks, the rod should take the strain by bending, and to do this it must not be too stiff, especially at the point. I think that most very small rods are too stiff, and although the automatic check on a thread-line reel to some extent makes up for this, I don't think it gives the tackle or the hold on the fish's mouth a fair chance. I think a reasonable-lengthed rod, at least 7 ft, is essential for bait fishing.

The use of very light tackle where salmon run big and the river is very rocky is a mistake as so many fish are lost through breaking; while the use of very strong tackle where the salmon run small spoils the sport, as they can be hauled in so quickly. There is no doubt that the greatest fun is to be had by catching salmon on fairly light tackle, when they cannot be caught on anything else.

I had some leave soon after finishing my flying training and a friend asked me to go and fish the Frome in Dorsetshire where he and some brother officers had taken a beat. I arrived at lunch-time one day to find a message that he couldn't get off until later but that I was to go to the hut and collect tackle and start fishing. I took his dog with me, now alas no more, and with the help of a diagram we found our way to the hut and opened it up. It was full of the tackle of six fishermen spread about in every direction, rods from about 2–20 feet, spinning, casting, prawning; tins of rotting prawns, fishing bags, rubber boots, reels, gaffs, everything that had ever been invented to catch salmon, mostly in a shocking state of dilapidation. I thought I had better stick to A's tackle, some of which I could recognise scattered about the hut. I found a rather second-hand Tweed bait tackle and some golden sprats which didn't smell too bad, but the only cast I could find was of twisted wire; however, I tested it well and it looked all right, so I put it on and sallied forth. There was a map of the river with the pools marked, on the wall, which I tried to memorise without success and I finally decided to fish the likely looking places. The Frome must be one of the smallest rivers with the largest fish in England, an excellent combination. A fish of 30–40 lbs is nothing uncommon and with the wind behind him I am sure a German soldier could spit across it, though God forbid that he would have the chance! I started off in a very likely-looking place, which I afterwards learnt had never held a fish, and worked my way downstream.

Although it was April it was very cold and my fingers soon became pretty numb, and when I was least expecting it there was a bang on the line which jerked the reel handle from my fingers. The line went quite slack, but when I had pulled myself together and wound in the loose line, he was there, a solid weight. He gave a couple of heavy tugs and then he came upstream past me, a great grey shape in the shallow water. The line made the swishing noise it does when trying to keep up with a fast-moving fish, and then the trace broke about 6 inches from the fish. The name of the pool I afterwards discovered was 'The Pulpit', but the language I used as I flung the remains of the trace into the river could never have been used from one.

The next day A. managed to get off and we went down to the river together. The prawns looked and smelt even worse than

The Loisach (Bavaria)

the day before, so A. left me at the mill pool near the top of the water, armed with a 12-ft fly rod and a spinning rod, while he went to try and get some more, as most fish at this time of year on the Frome are caught on prawns.

Water runs into the mill pool from the sluice and also from the end of the salmon ladder, a deep channel, about 20 yards away. The water from the sluice rushes down the pool, then back in a large whirlpool past the ladder, and back to the sluice where it joins the rush again. I began fishing with a fly from between the sluice and the ladder, the recognised place, but I did no good, so I went below where the ladder came in and fished up towards the main stream of water, the fly hanging in the backwater. I was using a greased line and a small double-hooked Blue Charm. The very last cast I was going to make the line moved away. I let the reel turn twice, then raised the rod point and I had him. The pool isn't more than 30 yards in diameter, and the fish tore around it, sometimes out in the white foaming water, where he jumped twice, the line entering the water alarmingly far below where he appeared, and sometimes in the deep water under my feet where the bank was overhanging. Once he hugged my bank and the line disappeared my side of the point between where I stood and the ladder. Then he jumped in the ladder, which shook me a bit, but he came out again with no worse result than covering the line with floating weed, which stayed there the rest of the time I was playing him. But worse was to follow as an enormous tree stump covered with roots and branches, which had been floating harmlessly at the side of the pool, decided to join in the fun and got itself into the middle of the whirlpool where it proceeded to go round and round. The fish bolted straight under the log and cruised up and down on the far side of the pool. I put my rod point right down under the water, when the line was passing under the stump, and luckily the fish kept fairly deep, but each time I felt it catch and then spring off. Eventually he began to tire, but he kept right out in the fast water where he lay against the line, letting the current press against him. I couldn't get him over into the slack at my side of the pool, and finally he was washed out of the tail of the pool, which was quite shallow and covered with great banks of weed, mostly just below the surface, but on it in places. By keeping my rod as high as possible, and exerting every ounce of strain that I thought the tackle would stand, I just managed to get his head towards me so that the current pressed him towards my bank, and I pulled him over the top of two large weed patches into a deep little hole by my bank. He tried to get out again but he was too tired and a moment later he came to the surface and I gaffed him. He weighed 19 lbs, which is small for the Frome, but it was quite big enough for me.

In this case there was an alternative which I could have tried when the fish looked like being washed out of the pool. I could have slackened off the line and hoped that when he felt the strain go he would swim back into the pool again. This often works when a salmon looks like leaving a pool, but if a fish is very nearly dead-beat it probably won't. Rightly or wrongly I thought that the fish was too tired to swim back against the stream. I believe if I had let him go he would have sunk down and drifted back with the current, which was very strong, until he found some slacker water among the weed beds.

There are times when one has to pull harder than one feels is really safe, and I had to do so to skittle a 19-lb salmon over two weed beds with a light salmon cast, but if he had got under the weeds on the far side of the stream, I should never have extracted him without going in after him, and he would probably have broken me. Later in the season another man lost three fish in one evening among those weeds.

In dry-fly fishing most fish are lost because they manage to get into weed patches. Now whenever I hook a trout on a chalk stream I exert the very maximum of strain from the first moment I feel him. Chalk-stream trout don't play as well as North-Country trout, but they are great strategicians and use every weed bed to the best advantage. If one can stop their original dash for cover the chances of landing them are much better, for even if they do get to a weed bed they won't be able to burrow in very deeply if a good strain is kept on them, and they will be easier to extract later. Some fish when hooked lose their heads and are easily dealt with, but the big fish who knows his water doesn't take much time to make up his mind where to go.

Strangely enough sea trout when hooked in the sea make no attempt to get into seaweed, they just rush about and jump, and if one is broken in seaweed it is pure bad luck. Presumably they don't regard seaweed as a means of escaping from their enemies and so it never enters their heads to use it when hooked, but if one hooks a 'cuddy'—a small fish either lythe or saith and usually about 4 to 6 inches long—he is into the seaweed like a knife wriggling in and out of the stems. If he is allowed any slack line it is impossible to get him out again without breaking even if one is using a 1x cast or even stronger. No cuddy could possibly hold on to seaweed with his mouth hard enough to break a 1x cast and there is no stream to help him, so how does he do it? Simply by weaving when he gets among the seaweed so that the line passes round many stems of seaweed before it pulls against him. I wouldn't dare to compare a cuddy to the noble stew-bred, fly-fed South Country trout, but I don't think that a trout grips weeds with its mouth any more than the cuddy does. I know I am on delicate ground as many people believe they do and some say they have actually seen it. A fish usually has his mouth open when being played, he also opens and shuts it slightly when breathing with it open and if he was seen doing this in a weed bed he might appear to be gripping the weeds; but if I was a trout I would try to use the weeds as a fulcrum and by altering course as I went into them, make the pull on myself less direct—just as the cuddy does with seaweed. Weeds are fairly tough things and as they are always in motion in a stream it makes it easier for the trout to wrap some round the cast. The thicker the weed bed the more difficult it is to get a trout out of it, whereas if it gripped the weeds in its mouth, it would only need as much weed as it could get into its mouth to make it as difficult as possible to dislodge. But whatever they do when they get into a weed bed, it is fairly easy to get a trout out again if a direct pull can be made from below. because the cast is lying in the same direction as the strands of weed and so is not wrapped over or under any, but from at right angles to the flow of water and some distance away it is usually impossible. Hand lining is also essential as a firmer and more direct pull can be exerted. If the weed-gripping theory is correct why should a direct pull from below be any more effective than any other? I may be wrong: but I shall only believe the other when I see it. Water plays funny tricks with light and it is often impossible to see exactly what is happening.

More fish are lost by being too light on them than by being too hard. My father always said that, and I am sure it is quite true. The beginner practically always makes the mistake of letting the fish have too much of its own way. There are many times when a fish is in complete control if it is any weight in comparison with the strength of the tackle, but whenever it rests for a moment the maximum strain should be exerted to keep it from regaining its strength.

The first big fish I played was a sea trout of 8 lbs on a 2x cast and 8 ft rod in Loch na Creitach in Skye. I was 9 years old. The fish took a floating teal and green. I played it for about half-an-hour, and then I was exhausted and my father, much against his will, had to take over, and I was appalled at the amount of strain he put on it with my little rod. I didn't think the rod would take it, let alone the cast. The increased strain made the fish fight much harder and left it no peace when it tried to rest, and he landed it ten minutes later; but my father had done more to tire the fish in ten minutes than I had done in half-an-hour.

One can go to the other extreme and pull hard enough to break the tackle, but this very seldom happens if the tackle is kept in decent condition and constantly tested. I think I have only seen it done once and the culprit was my father who was fishing with a new 2x cast and a fly I had tied. He hooked a large sea trout in Coruisk and as usual pulled it very hard, but for once he pulled too hard. I thought he was giving it too much stick, but I didn't say anything. I wasn't a bit surprised when the cast broke. He couldn't understand it and when I said I thought he had just pulled too hard he said 'Did I?' in amazement.

When playing sea trout the most dangerous time of all is immediately after the fish is hooked, for generally as soon as a sea trout feels a hook he is off like a bullet and if there is any slack line and it gets caught round one's fingers or a button it means being broken. I have so often seen it happen. The rod is pulled straight and springs back so quickly that it just seems to flick down, but the fish gets a direct pull and will break any strength of cast. The buttons of the cuffs of a coat are a great danger and should be swiftly cut off before they can cause any damage, if one is fishing from a boat and working the fly in close by pulling a lot of line in through the rings of the rod.

They are quickest off the mark if hooked at night when they are in fairly shallow water. I was fishing from the bank one night with the check on my reel rather light as one of the springs had broken; but it served well enough if one kept a finger on the line while playing a fish. It was getting fairly dark, when I hooked something close in shore which shot out from the shallow so fast that my reel overran and I was immediately broken.

One of the commonest reasons for losing sea trout is that people fish without enough line on their reels. One should have 100 yards, 40 of line and 60 of backing, and even then it may be necessary to follow a big fish in a boat.

Sea trout usually jump when they are being played and a half-pounder fresh from the sea may spend most of the time in the air. The rule is that the rod point should be lowered and the line slackened when a fish jumps as the fish may fall back on the cast and break it if it is kept tight. It is advisable to do so even with small fish, as if they are not heavy enough to break the cast, and don't fall directly on it, the jar of hitting the water is often enough to tear the hook from its hold in the fish's mouth. I have tried both lowering the point and not lowering it and I am in no doubt that one loses far more small fish if the line is kept taut when they jump. To land the greatest number of small sea trout, under a pound, it is definitely best to play them gently even if fishing with strong tackle, as their mouths are so soft and the hold is so apt to break.

The amount one can pull at a sea trout depends on the size of the fly and the size of the fish, within the limits of the strength of the tackle. If a large fish is lightly hooked, it is just as likely to get off if played very gently as if it is played fairly hard, as it will have to be played for so much longer. The size of the hook is also a most important consideration, as a fairly large fly is more likely to have a good hold on the fish's mouth than a very small one. For the playing point of view there is an optimum size of hook for each size of fish.

It often happens that sea trout only take well for a comparatively short time during the day, and if they suddenly come on, no time should be wasted in playing the fish, especially if two people are fishing from the same boat. It is a mistake to try and hurry a fish out of consideration for someone else, but if it is a large fish, say over 6 lbs a good strain should be kept on him all the time. If he is lost not much time has been wasted and if he is landed there is the chance of another before they go off the take. This is especially true of night fishing when the rise may only last for about an hour, as it is easy enough to play an 8 lb fish for an hour unless a good strain is kept on it all the time.

I remember playing a fish for about 45 minutes one evening, and he eventually broke me. Just at the break the cast was badly frayed, so probably the fish was hooked in the tongue and the gut had frayed on its teeth. My brother was justly annoyed that I had wasted so much time with nothing to show for it. I was young at the time and still frightened of pulling a fish hard enough, but if I had put enough strain on him to land him in half-an-hour all would have been well. Since then I have often landed a large sea trout after twenty minutes or so and found the cast practically frayed through; a few more minutes and it would have broken. After landing a sizable fish or a number of small ones it is always worth looking at the cast just above the fly. If it is at all frayed the fly should be broken off and tied on again above the frayed piece of cast.

Many people don't know how to pull at a fish and old books

give the wrong impression. I have even quite recently read about 'giving him the butt'. One might just as well give him a packet of cigarettes for all the damage it does. The maximum strain is exerted by pointing the rod straight at the fish and reeling in; no tackle will stand it. The minimum strain is exerted by having as much bend as possible in the rod, and the lightest check on the reel. 'Giving him the butt' means bending the rod as much as possible, if it means anything. The greatest strain consistent with safety is to have the rod at about 45° to the water and a strong check on the reel. I prefer a fairly strong check which I increase with the forefinger of my left hand whenever the fish tries to rest. After hooking a sea trout in a loch, I try to judge its size fairly quickly and set the check on my reel accordingly; the bigger the fish the stronger the check, always within the limit of the strength of my cast. With a bit of practice one can make a fair guess at the size of a fish even if one doesn't see it take or jump soon after. I think one can feel the motions it makes to swim if it is under 4 or 5 lbs, and over that one just feels a steady strain; but sea trout are usually most accommodating and jump soon after they are hooked.

I have noticed recently that most salmon that are hooked in the tongue jump when they are being played, but practically all sea trout jump unless they have been in fresh water a very long time. If there is any doubt about whether one has hooked a salmon or a sea trout it is at once settled if the fish jumps, just as surely as by counting the scales between the adipose fin and the lateral line. A salmon jumps sideways and leaves the water at an angle of 20° or so, while a sea trout jumps straight up in the air. One can sometimes hear a purr made by its tail, which continues to flap when it is in the air.

After a fish has been exhausted by being played it has to be induced to leave its natural element and live, for a short while, on the land. Salmon are usually gaffed, but I have not had much experience of this. The first fish I gaffed was a kelt which was rather a black! Luckily nobody was in sight and I launched it again and it swam away; but I don't think its expectation of life was very good; however, I don't suppose I am the only person who has gaffed a kelt. When I did have to gaff my own salmon I remembered to put the gaff behind the line, the one and only golden rule, and I was surprised how easily a sharp gaff slid into the fish, no jerk being necessary, only a smooth pull. Gaffing one's own salmon is rather like stalking without a stalker. I always get very excited when playing and gaffing a fish by myself.

There are different rules on different rivers about the use of a gaff, mostly designed to prevent kelts being gaffed, and in some rivers a gaff is hardly ever used. Fish are almost entirely netted on the Tweed. Fishing with a ghillie this is a safer and quicker method; but it is almost impossible to wield a salmon net by oneself. There was an objection to using a net when people fished with bait and minnow tackles, which had bunches of triangles sticking out in every direction, as one of the triangles might catch in the net and break the tackle or the hold on the fish; but it has now been realised that one or two triangles are enough for the best and biggest of salmon. Most fishermen no longer fling potential barbed wire entanglements into rivers for the alluring of fish.

If one is netting a trout oneself it is safe to move the net towards the fish, at the same time pulling the fish over the net; but if someone else is using the net who hasn't much experience, it is best for the net to be kept still and the fish pulled over it. Any sudden sweep with the net should be avoided as the fish can and will move much faster. A good man with a net may move it but he will wait until he is certain of landing the fish.

It is sometimes possible to land a fish before it is absolutely played out, as it will often come to the surface before it is dead-beat and stay there for a moment. A sea trout can usually be pulled a few feet along the surface before it decides to make another dash. To take advantage of this it is best to keep the fish's head out of water as much as possible and try to get the net under it before it makes off again, as I don't believe a fish can see with its eyes out of water. This chance won't occur if the fish has seen the boat and it certainly won't after it has seen the net.

Problems sometimes arise about landing a large fish in a small and often rotten landing net. This shouldn't happen if one was always properly equipped, but one sometimes isn't, especially fishing for sea trout if a salmon is hooked. If it seems doubtful whether a fish will fit into a net when fishing from a boat, it is usually best to land and conduct the final scene from firm ground. There are gaff heads which screw into the same shaft as a landing-net head and amazingly enough most trout landing-net shafts have the same sized thread, but this should be checked up before going fishing and not when one has hooked the fish of a lifetime and is trying frantically to unscrew the net to screw in the gaff. I always carry one of these gaff heads now, but I had to learn by bitter experience.

I was fishing a loch in Skye and the only net in the boat was just about big enough for a 10 lb sea trout. I had caught a few but none of any size, and towards the end of a drift the ghillie said 'I wish Mister Stephen could hook a big one'; for once it worked. The usual size of salmon in Skye is 6–10 lbs, but my father had put down some parr of a larger strain a few years before. The next cast after the ghillie's remark, almost as soon as the fly landed, the large head and shoulder of a fish appeared. I struck and had him on. He jumped a moment later, sideways out of the water as a salmon will, and I saw the silver pink colour of a fresh fish. I estimated his weight at about 18 lbs and also realised that I had struck far too quickly for a salmon. I was lucky to have him on at all, and I knew that he probably wasn't very firmly hooked. I was fishing with a 10-ft rod and a 1x cast, so I had every chance of tiring him fairly quickly. The bottom of the loch was rock and small stones with no snags, but he immediately ran out into about 60 ft of water and made no attempt to go deep, so there was never any danger of being broken round a rock. He played very hard and at the end of 20 minutes he was nearly exhausted. We had decided to land to tail him from the shore as soon as he was ready and we were thinking of moving in. He came to the surface nearly done, but he saw the boat and made another short run. The water was absolutely clear and we could see his every movement as he swam against the taut line, but he couldn't keep it up and he came to the surface again about 8 ft from the boat. He was absolutely done now and as salmon will he rolled slowly over on to his side and lay still on the surface. As he did so the hold gave and he was off. There was nothing we could do but watch him sink, which he did very slowly on his side without moving a fin until he became indistinct and finally disappeared into the green depth. I have carried a gaff or a gaff-head ever since that day, but I have never had occasion to use it.

I have heard arguments whether it is better to put the fish's head or tail into the net if it isn't large enough for the whole fish. The fish's centre of gravity is well forward and it usually swims forwards, so it is best to get its head well in and hope for the best, with sea trout which can't be tailed. Salmon can be tailed, and should be, although one has to be a bit of an acrobat to tail one's own salmon with one hand and keep a strain on it with the rod in the other. Incidentally a hat is a very poor substitute for a landing-net, because as the hat is lifted water runs out of it which washes the fish out as well! It is fairly easy to beach a trout on shingle that slopes gently into the water. If a fair strain is kept on the fish every time it kicks it slips a little further up the shingle until one can get between it and the river and pick it up.

Once the fish is on the land it is a mistake to let it get back into the water after it has been unhooked but this quite often happens. One of the favourite ways is to try to hit its head on the gunwale of a boat. The fish gives a wriggle and slips out of one's hands and back into the loch. Another good way of doing it is by trying to put a live fish into a basket when wading in deep water; either kill the fish or go ashore before trying to unhook it and transfer it from the net to the basket. I think my younger brother will always do this since he inadvertently put a fish of about 1½ lbs back into the Eamont. He was cross enough an hour or so later when I saw him so I hate to think of what he said at the time.

CHAPTER IV

AUTUMN SALMON FISHING

TWEED in autumn. The bright days with a warm sun, and hoar frost in the shadows until mid-morning; the trees, with leaves already turned and beginning to fall, standing out against the blue sky; the water as clear and fresh as liquid silver breaking white over rocks or reflecting every colour of the sky and autumn as it flows smooth through open fields and deep through woods.

The sound of it just heard before the river comes in sight, gently murmuring in the distance but getting louder as one approaches. All the little noises of water pushing round and over stones, meeting other waters in the restless certainty of reaching the sea. And what of the smell? The scents of an autumn morning, crisp and clean, with fallen leaves, a distant bonfire, and the freshness of the river. It is cooler near the river with the scents of water and all the plants that grow by it in the air. The good autumn days are among the best of the year. With these surroundings and a salmon rod in one's hands, how could a day be anything but well spent.

I once motored from Perth for a day's fishing on the Tweed, starting after duty on the day before and staying the night in Edinburgh. The guns were firing as I crossed the ferry and drove along the dark road towards the town. Only their flashes lit up the night. I started early next morning and as I crossed the Lammermuirs the ice was still on the puddles while hoar frost sparkled on heather and bent. From the summit, every hill of the wild border country right to the Cheviots was clear-cut against the pale blue of a cold dawn.

I arrived at my brother's house at nine, in time for a breakfast of porridge and cream, eggs and bacon, toast and marmalade. We discussed the chances of catching a fish over it. The river was fairly low but there were some fish in it and a few were still coming through, so the chances seemed quite good. The boat was waiting at the Orchard, and as we put the rod up I saw two fish move in the fast water at the head of the pool which filled me with hopeful expectation. Only flies are allowed on the Tweed after October 1st, so I started fishing with a small Mar Lodge. It is great to feel the weight and strength of a salmon rod in one's hands again and to get into the rhythm of casting so that the line falls true and straight on the water at the right angle, then the fly beyond it with a little plop. The Orchard is a lovely pool in a fairly low water, shallow at the top and deepening out towards the end. A fish took half-way down the pool with a firm draw. That second when 'he's there' is surely the most thrilling of all in fishing. There are some ledges of rock in the Orchard, but he avoided them, and shortly afterwards we landed him, a clean-looking fish of 13 lbs that couldn't have been in the river for long.

After lunch I hooked a large dark fish in Elsie just in the glide at the tail of the pool. We manoeuvred him up into the pool, where he jumped and showed himself, but he got off a few minutes later. The day changed and became darker after that, and I didn't move another fish, but my brother who took the rod to fish the 'Laird's cast' had hold of a fish for a moment and moved yet another.

Not a great day perhaps, but worth anything as I hadn't fished for several months, and it was 'stolen', for who ever heard of motoring from Perth to the Tweed for a day's fishing in war-time. It was dark by the time I reached Edinburgh on the way back, and I had to drive the rest of the way with only the feeble glow of a war-time headlight to show the road which was strange to me; but the sound of the river was still in my ears and the rippling of water before my eyes.

Autumn salmon in the Tweed average around 16 lbs and are much bigger than the spring salmon which are mostly about 7 lbs, and they have a different appearance. I have looked through all the literature I can find but I have discovered no definite 'gen' as to whether they are separate breeds or not. The spring fish spawn about October and the autumn fish in January but they probably overlap. Do the spring fish breed only spring

Playing and Landing a salmon on the Tweed

fish and the autumn ones only autumn fish? I have never examined any scales of Tweed fish, as I thought the picture must be quite clear on such an important river.

Why and when do salmon take a fly? Hundreds of people have written thousands of words about this without getting much nearer the answer. The state of the water and the number of fish in it are much the most important factors; but entirely from a weather point of view, what is the best day for fishing? Everybody has his own idea of the perfect day for salmon fishing, because it was under these conditions that he caught most fish or had a good day, and I believe that if one took all these days and mixed them together and took the average or 'mean' day one would have the answer. The day might be fairly warm for the time of year with occasional gleams of sun and a gentle breeze from the South West. It would be a nice day to go fishing anyway and not likely to aggravate one's rheumatics. I think that if a day improves towards this perfect day the chances of hooking a fish increase, and if the day becomes less like it the chances also become less.

The first autumn of the war, I took Sprouston on the Tweed for the second fortnight in October. Three days before we began there was a good spate after a long drought and plenty of fish came up. We arrived on a bright sunny day to find the 'Cottage Stream' full of fish. My brother fished it in the morning while I fished above, but he did no good and in the afternoon we changed round. I jokingly said at lunch that he could fish it again after I had caught two out of it. There had been a bright sun all morning, but soon after lunch a few clouds came up and the sun went in for short periods. I was half-way down the cast when the sun first went in and within five minutes I was fast in a fish. We went ashore to play and land him. He weighed 17 lbs. Ten minutes later I hooked another and landed it also, a fish of 16 lbs, both wonderfully fresh for autumn salmon, one with sea lice. They both took a 'yellow dog' on a No. 3 hook. I went for my brother and we changed round again, but by the time he started fishing the sky had cleared and he never moved a fish although they were showing all down each side of the stream.

Everyone who has fished for salmon can surely think of examples of this kind. The wind drops for a moment from a gale to a gentle zephyr and a fish takes; or the day lightens and the sun comes out for a moment and a fish is hooked.

Sprouston is an interesting beat to fish because, besides the usual runs in which salmon are caught, there is the Dub which often holds a great many fish. There are quite a few 'dubs' on the Tweed, broad fairly slow-flowing stretches of water usually just above a cauld or weir. The Sprouston Dub is one of the best on the Tweed. The boat has to be worked from the bottom to the top or the flow of water is insufficient to bring the fly round fast enough, and there must be a breeze before it is worth fishing it with a fly. I fished there one day when there was a light variable breeze. Peter Young thought there wasn't much chance, but I had fished 'Little Davie' all morning without a sign of a fish, and there were several showing in the Dub so we went to try it. There were little patches of water being ruffled by the wind, but they never seemed to be near the boat, and most of the time I was fishing in a glassy calm, only broken by my line falling on it and occasionally by a moving fish. After about an hour a gust of wind hit the water just where I was fishing, while the whole of the rest of the Dub was quite calm. As the fly came round I said jokingly 'This is our chance', and Peter said it wasn't a very good one; but to our amazement the line tightened and I hooked and landed a fish of 13 lbs.

'Little Davie' is one of the finest runs on the Tweed, but fish lie in rather different places in autumn to their spring lies and we saw very few fish move in it, only catching four in the fortnight, two of which were spring fish, very thin and greenish in colour. My mother was always intrigued by the name and wondered whether Little Davie had caught his first fish in it or been drowned there, until we discovered that he was a boatman after whom it was named. I remember the first fish I caught in it was on a bright frosty morning without a cloud in the sky. It was very cold when we started, with a hard frost and rather foggy, but by mid-morning it had cleared out into a brilliant day with a hot sun shining up the river. I was fishing with a Silver

Wilkinson from the left bank sitting in the boat while Peter let it down from the shore. The bank is fairly steep and high with gorse bushes growing on it, which makes casting from the shore difficult. It is a lovely run and the fly works beautifully. When I first started I expected a pull every cast, but I was disillusioned by this time. He took well out in the stream with a determined pull, and the rod bent to his weight. He played in the rough water all the time and once I was afraid he might go out of the bottom of the pool, but he came back again and we landed him after about twenty minutes, a lovely clean fish of 20 lbs, with the pink flush of a really fresh salmon.

There are two other places on Sprouston in which fish are caught, but where one would never dream of fishing unless one knew about them. They are both called 'The Hole'. The bottom one is opposite the cottage stream, right under the bank. There is practically no stream and it is only about 15 yards in diameter. The fish following the main flow of the river, which is the way of salmon, don't pass within 50 yards of it, but somehow salmon get into it and stay there for a time. When we were fishing the Cottage Stream we always kept an eye on it. We generally saw one or two salmon show in the hole and they quite often took. As there is no stream a new technique has been devised to fish these places. A very short line is cast out of one side of the stern of the boat and 'led' round to the other side with the rod point; then the performance is repeated—have you ever heard of a more unlikely way of catching a fish? But it quite often works. I came down from Little Davie one day to find my brother slowly rowing away from the hole tight in something which he was towing along behind the boat. They brought it right through the Cottage Stream to the bank where I was standing, and I took photographs with a cine-camera while he played and landed it, a lovely fish of 24 lbs, as bright as a spring fish. A few days later he caught one of 32 lbs from the same place although it could hardly have had room to turn round in it, and these were the two largest fish we caught while we had the beat.

I never did any good in this hole, but I fished the top one, above the Dub one day. The first cast something just touched the fly. The river was full of leaves; but it didn't feel quite like a leaf, so I cast again, and again I felt a slight check as I led the fly around the stern of the boat, but there was no sign of a swirl in the water. This happened a third time, but the fourth time he grabbed it properly and I had him. He wasn't quite so clean as some of the fish but still quite good for autumn, when the fish are usually redder than the spring fish. He weighed 19 lbs.

One of the disadvantages to autumn fishing is the great number of leaves that come down the river if there is a hard frost followed by a wind and a rise in the water. Strangely enough it doesn't seem to make much difference to the fish taking and they will take a 'yellow dog', which is much the same colour as a leaf, even when the river is so full of leaves that the fly must be practically invisible. The trouble is that leaves are always being caught on the fly and if they come down sufficiently thick it may be impossible to fish. We were stopped one or two days by a big coloured water and too many leaves. Fish will often take a large fly when the water is very coloured. One day the next season my brother caught three fish and he was the only man fishing on the whole Tweed that day as the water was so big and coloured that nobody else thought it worth a try. He only went down as it was near the end of the season and he only had the one day.

The favourite fly on the Tweed in the autumn is probably the 'yellow dog' or Garry. I have never seen one for sale anywhere else than in Forrest's shop in Kelso. London shops I have asked have never even heard of it. It has a black floss silk body with silver tinsel, a jay hackle and the wing is of polar-bear fur, mostly dyed yellow but with a streak of red in it. I suppose it was originally made from somebody's yellow dog, and when it was first discovered I expect golden labradors had to be pretty careful or they found themselves being plucked to make flies, as it certainly is an amazingly effective fly in autumn and early spring. It isn't so popular as a small summer fly, as for some reason fish seldom take it so well then; but there are days when fish will take it in the summer and look at nothing else. It is not unlike the Torrish, which has some silver on the body, is a rather neater-looking fly, and can be found decorating any London shop.

The design of salmon flies has come a long way since Scrope spent days and nights fishing for salmon on the Tweed, and pitched his tent on the bank, to the consternation of his host who thought the sight of it might prevent the fish from running until Scrope proved by lines 'adroitly drawn' that it was invisible from the river. If I remember right a snowstorm blew it away that night, but they were tough in those days and Scrope never wore waders, cutting holes in his boots to let the water out. He is careful to point out that he didn't mind the water but he didn't like the noise it made in his boots as he walked along the bank. In spring when the temperature was below freezing and the water rather cold, he advised anglers to look at the colour of their legs from time to time, and if they were only 'rubicund' it was all right to go on fishing, but if they were black it was advisable to go ashore for a bit!

The flies used in those days were very sombre by comparison with our modern patterns, and they mostly had well-fluffed-out wool bodies, dark hackles and a mallard or turkey wing. I tied some of Scrope's flies the other day from a coloured plate in his book, but I haven't had a chance to try them out yet. He says that if a fish is risen on one of these flies, but doesn't take a hold, and another particular pattern is put over it, the fish will almost invariably take the second. It would be very interesting to see if this still holds on the Tweed and if I get an opportunity of a day's fishing after the war I shall certainly try it out.

The flies used on the Eden in Cumberland at about the same time were very similar; but they used to catch a great many fish on them.

Towards the end of November the autumn fish are apt to become rather red, although fresh autumn fish and an occasional spring fish are still coming through. The females are called Baggots and the males Kippers, perhaps because they are generally larger and they do kipper so well. The larger fish are fairly coarse in the texture of the flesh, but when they are salted and smoked they are transformed into delicious smoked salmon. When we were fishing Sprouston we had most of the larger fish kippered, and besides eating them ourselves most of the winter, I sent pieces to my friends as Christmas presents, but in those days lemons were plentiful in the land. Quite recently my brother sent me a piece and I had it for dinner in the mess with a few friends on several occasions; luckily there was only about one helping left when I was shot down, although there were two brace of pheasants and a duck, which we had shot the day before, in the back of my car.

The size of flies used in the autumn varies with the height and colour of the water. When the river becomes low and clear a greased line and small fly often rises a fish which wouldn't look at a sunk fly, just as in the summertime when the water becomes low and warm. On my last leave in October I had a few days' fishing on the Tweed. Most of the time the water was low and clear although there were quite a number of fish about. There was some rain one evening, but in the morning the river hadn't risen when I started fishing the long stream on Rutherford. At the top of the stream behind the island the water was fairly heavy so I began fishing with a sunk line and a fairly large fly. There was half a gale of wind blowing, but luckily it was downstream and although it made it very hard work for Brown rowing the boat, it was quite possible to fish. I managed to knock a couple of lovely new flies off by hitting them against the top of the rod during the forward cast, which it is very easy to do in a strong wind.

We saw one or two fish move and half-way down the island there was a swirl at my fly, but he didn't touch me and wouldn't come again. Towards the bottom of the pool I had a heavy pull, but he was gone before I could raise the rod point, which was disappointing. Below the island the river widens out and is rather slower running, so I changed rods and began fishing with a greased line. Brown said: 'He should be here, Mr Steve,' and a moment later he was, for the line moved smoothly away across the surface. I let him have the slack line I held in my hand, but before he had taken it all up he let go and I never felt him. We found when we got down to the guage by Brown's house that the river had risen several inches and this probably accounted for the fish taking so very short and only gripping the feathers of the fly for a moment.

The 'slap' was in perfect order and I fished it down with both rods, but without success. We didn't even see a fish move in it, but 'between the caulds' was slightly sheltered from the west wind and full of fish which were continually showing down both sides of the run. Flocks of mallard were flying up the river all day, beating slowly against the wind and wheeling off when they sighted the boat, the drakes' plumage showing up brilliantly in the clear light. The sun came out in gleams and it was quite warm out of the wind. It seemed a good chance, but the river must have been rising too rapidly, for I never touched or moved a fish here or in the pools below, and my brother who fished it later in the afternoon didn't move one either. Although I never caught a fish that day it was very enjoyable fishing with Brown again and learning more about the river; besides I moved several fish and there is a thrill in this even if one doesn't hook one.

The last day I had was on Makerston. The river had run in again, so I fished all the time with a greased line. We went down to 'the Daws' first as there were quite a number of fish in it. This is a fascinating spot with a tumble of water above and below the pool, and the loud sound of falling water always in the air. At the head of the pool the water is rough and broken, but the main pool and the tail is a smooth glide among slabs of rock. It is here that most of the fish are caught.

We saw quite a few moving in the smooth water while we were putting up the rod and fishing the top half of the pool. One moved twice just above a rock which divides the flow of water in two, and when we reached the place the line moved away practically as soon as the fly touched the water; it can't have sunk more than a few inches, but the fish never broke the surface. I let go the slack I was holding, and this time there was no mistake: he took it all and came on to the rod with a firm pull.

I raised the point and had him on. We were fairly near the tail of the pool but he made no attempt to leave it and played well up in the middle. When he was nearly done we rowed ashore and I stepped out of the boat on to the bank, a rather tricky proceeding holding a 14 ft rod and keeping a steady strain on a fish. A salmon is always very unwilling to leave the fast water and come into the slack at the side of a pool. This fish played well out in the strong stream until he was nearly beat. At last I was able to bring him into the shore. He only made one more short run before he was netted, a nice fish of 19 lbs.

There were one or two fish showing in 'Elsie', but they were mostly fairly dark coloured and had been in the water a long time. In the slap at the tail of the pool a fish just broke the water as he rose at the fly, but he never touched it and I let the fly come on round without casting again. We rowed up a few yards to come down on him again, and I left the fly trailing in the water behind the boat as we went up. When we were high enough I started casting. Just as I took the fly out of the water a fish swirled at it. I think it was probably the same fish which had turned and followed the fly after missing it further down, but it was impossible to say, although he didn't come again when we reached the spot where he had first risen.

My brother and Jane brought the lunch down and we had a picnic together. In the afternoon my brother went to fish the Daws again while Jane and I went for a walk. We arrived back just as he hooked a fish in the extreme tail of the pool where the water hung before rushing into a narrow trough of breaking water between slabs of rock. They said it looked a very big fish as it took. It plunged down and gave one or two heavy tugs before the strain on the line became a dead pull. Nothing they could do would shift it. They tried landing on both ledges of rock and pulling it from above and below but they never felt the fish move again, only a dead strain, and eventually they had to break the line. The fish must have dived through a hole among the boulders deep below the surface, and somehow managed to wedge the line between two rocks. It is very nearly as exciting watching a friend play a fish as playing it oneself, and quite as agonising to see a salmon being lost without being able to do anything about it. I was jumping up and down on the nearest point to the boat that I could reach without getting my feet wet, all the time they were trying to dislodge the fish.

CHAPTER V

SPRING SALMON

SPRING fishing has quite another charm. Rivers are different and have a colder colour as they run through the bare countryside before the grass begins to grow. One expects roaring spates of foaming water with arctic winds and snow on the hills. It is no time for the fair-weather sportsman when drops of water freeze on the rings of the rod, and the wind comes like a knife from the snowfields of the high hills; but the reward is a spring salmon, by far the most satisfactory catch for any fisherman. There is a Gaelic saying that only a child, a woodcock and a salmon are beautiful in death. The author must have been thinking of the pinkish flush on the clear silver of a salmon fresh from the Atlantic sea.

My first leave during the war was after the 5th Btn. of the Scots Guards was disbanded in March 1940. It wasn't really deserved, as it became later when I joined the R.A.F., but it came after a very pleasant skiing expedition to Chamonix with the minimum of military discipline, and after my leave I returned to civilian life. We had a very good time in Chamonix as our section were all old friends. After we were disbanded the rest of them returned to their old regiments, but we all had ten days' leave and four of us decided it would be an excellent plan to go and catch a spring salmon. We had no time to take a beat on a river, so we decided to go to Altnaharra in Sutherland.

Phillip went there a day before the rest of us. We arrived one evening to find he had caught two fish that day out of Loch Naver: one was 12 lbs and the other 24 lbs, a very big fish for the loch, and we were filled with enthusiasm for the morrow. The weather was very cold most of the time with fairly frequent snow showers and only the spring note of the curlew to remind us that winter was really over. Fishing on the loch was a very chilly business, as at this time of year it is all trolling, but there was still a tremendous thrill about feeling the first salmon of the season. We usually fished with two or three rods behind each boat and only about twenty yards of line out, with a light weight, as the loch is quite shallow where the salmon lie. The best baits were a wagtail or a golden sprat cut down to make it very thin so that it spun fairly quickly.

There were quite a number of fish up and we seldom had a blank day. My best day was four fish from 8 to 12 lbs, but it was rather monotonous sitting and waiting for something to happen and I used to take turns at rowing to keep myself warm.

The hotel was very warm and comfortable to return to after a cold day's fishing on the loch. We entered our catches in the same game book that my mother and father used on their honeymoon thirty-three years before. The salmon were all fresh and excellent eating, and we had them grilled or boiled for most meals.

The river Mudale runs into Loch Naver by the hotel, and Willie Ross the ghillie had caught a fish out of it a fortnight before we arrived, so we thought it was probably quite a good chance. We usually fished it in the evening, after a day on the loch and a good tea to warm us up again, as the best pools were quite near the hotel, but I spent one whole day on it. Willie and I started after breakfast with our lunch in our pockets and we fished the whole river (which is about six miles long) from the bottom to the top and back again. Willie took his 'wand', which was a 12-ft greenheart, and I had a strong 10-ft sea-trout rod. The river runs through fairly flat boggy country and there was no shelter from the bitterly cold wind and frequent snow showers. The country was looking as bleak and desolate as only Sutherland can in a cold late spring. The distant hills were covered with snow and the sky was a dark grey with occasional breaks of greenish blue and gleams of watery sunshine. The heather and grass were still the brown of winter, with an occasional sheep showing white against it.

We fished alternate pools, Willie leaving me the best places, with instructions as to where to fish, and going on to the next pool himself. He set a great pace. Part of the time I froze when

I was fishing, while the rest I was sweating to try to catch him up. We had lunch sheltering behind a low stone wall, as a particularly bad snowstorm blew over, leaving the moor with a sprinkling of white on grass and heather. After lunch we fished on up as far as some falls and then turned for home, only fishing the best places on the way back; but as we passed pools Willie told me of fish that had been hooked, lost and landed in them, probably for the last twenty years, as he had been fishing there ever since he returned from serving in the Lovat Scouts in the last war and he had the retentive memory of a very keen fisherman. I asked him about the largest fish he had ever seen. It was a sad tale. A gentleman had hooked a monstrous salmon in a pool on the river Naver. Willie couldn't even make a guess at its weight although he had seen it clearly several times while it was being played. The gentleman played the fish for many hours, but he had a wife and she wore the pants, for when it was time to go home for tea she said so in no uncertain voice 'and the gentleman cut the line and left the fish'. There was no doubt by the tone in which Willie said it as to which of the two, his wife or the fish, he should have left. I am sure Willie thinks that a man can marry a wife any day, but perhaps only one day in a lifetime is there a chance of landing a record salmon. He is the keenest fisherman I have ever met, and although we had a blank day on the Mudale it was a pleasure spending it with him.

The rule about not fishing on Sunday is rather hard to observe when leave is difficult to get and of such short duration. As Philip's last day was on a Sunday it made it almost impossible. He put a rod down his trouser leg and we went for a walk after lunch. He walked rather stiffly at first until we were out of sight of the houses, and then we made our way down to the river by devious routes: but although we saw a fish move, our ungodliness must have been frowned upon, because we didn't rise anything, and in fact we never did catch a fish out of the Mudale during our stay at Altnaharra.

We were very kindly given a few days on the river Naver, which was a pleasant change from sitting in a boat on the loch. It is a lovely river with a series of good pools with fast rough water between them. As it is chiefly fed from the loch it never becomes very much coloured however large it may be, which is a great advantage. For the top part it runs through heathery and boggy country, but nearer the sea there are fields and occasional cottages along the banks. It is a fairly wide river and one can just cover it all fishing from the bank with waders, but it is an advantage to have a big rod. Only fly fishing is permitted. The local people use the most enormous and sinister-looking specimens; I have never seen anything like them before or since. We had no flies with us which were nearly big enough or shaggy enough by their standards; but our host kindly lent us some great hairy monsters, made from the downy part of the feather and tied on 8.0 or 9.0 hooks. Luckily I had an 18-ft rod and some strong casts with which to coax these super dragon-flies through the air.

The first day Philip and I had we shared a rod, but not knowing the water was a great handicap although we were told which parts to fish. We had a pleasant day but we only managed to catch a number of kelts. The second day Philip fished one beat and I fished the bottom beat, and Willie Ross insisted on coming with me for the day's outing. As he knew the water very well he was quite invaluable. There is a road down the valley, and when there is plenty of petrol in the land it is easier to use a car to go from pool to pool, but we had none, so we walked. If we wanted to fish the whole beat thoroughly, there was no time to be lost between pools, and Willie was always away to the next pool at a terrific pace before I could get my line wound in from the last cast in the previous pool. As I was wearing waders and he wasn't, I became very hot trying to keep up with him. I have never seen any other ghillie half as keen on catching a salmon. We fished a series of lovely pools without success until lunch time, and then towards the bottom of a fairly slow deep run I felt something touch the fly. I left it, expecting to feel the line tighten, but nothing else happened, so after a few seconds I raised the rod point thinking the fish had gone, but the rod bent the line running taut and straight into the water, and I felt that wonderful heavy jug-jog which means a salmon has been hooked.

I thought he was a kelt at first as the pool was sluggish, but he played pretty hard and when we saw him near the surface we found he was a clean fish; the excitement on my part was intense. Willie gaffed him expertly after about ten minutes and we found he weighed 10 lbs. He had the enormous furry fly as far down towards his stomach as it would go. He couldn't have swallowed it right down as it was too big, but he had tried his level best.

I made Willie try the pool down again while I had my lunch and he tried one or two other spots which could be reached from the bank. It was a pleasure to see him fishing. He threw a lovely line without any effort although he was fishing with a strange rod, but he was unlucky and didn't hook anything but a few kelts.

I can still remember the bottom pool of all. It was fairly broad and the glide at the tail was the best chance. I waded out as gently as possible to avoid sending ripples right across the smooth surface of the river, and fished it down carefully two steps at a time. We were near the sea and could smell the salt in the air. The sun came out for a time and made it quite warm. The cry of curlews and oyster-catchers was in the air as they flew up the river and were startled by us. The grass in the fields was beginning to grow and showed green in places among the dead yellow of winter. We saw two or three fish move and it looked a good chance but I never moved a thing. Willie told me that it fished better from the far side if one could get round by car, as however carefully one waded out it seemed to disturb the fish.

We worked our way upstream again after that, and in one pool I hooked three fish but they were all kelts. Kelts will be together in one pool, and the next day it may be quite clear of them while another pool is full. Fresh fish seem to keep clear of pools which are holding kelts. We had seen a few fresh fish move in one pool on our way down, so we made for it fairly quickly with just a few casts into the most likely spots in the other pools as we passed. This particular pool was at a bend in the river, with the stream coming across to our bank and running strongly down it for the last half of the pool. There was a high shingle bank behind, which made it difficult to cast, especially at the top of the pool where the stream and the lie of the salmon was well over, making a long line necessary. I thought I was doing quite nicely. After a dozen casts or so the line drew away and I felt a fish hard, then he was gone. I reeled in to look at the fly and found to my disgust that I had knocked the point of the hook off on the stone bank behind me.

This was very disappointing as it was only the second offer I had had the whole day. I tied on another fly and went on fishing without much hope as I had passed the place where we had seen the fish move earlier on. At the very end of the pool the line tightened again and I was into a fish. There was no doubt he was fresh as he jumped almost at once and showed himself a thick clean fish of about 15 lbs. He played very hard in the tail of the pool where the water began to run faster, and I couldn't make him come up into the stiller water above. I tried walking him up and he would follow for a way, but then he would run back and nothing I could do would stop him. I also tried getting below him to make him swim upstream against the strain, but I lost even more ground that way. It wasn't very long before he decided to leave the pool altogether. He kept well out in the middle of the river and went downstream among the white broken water and stones. I had to run down to get opposite him and then hold my rod as high as possible to prevent the line between myself and the fish getting round a stone—'drowned and cut' as Scrope describes it. For about 200 yards the water was very rough and broken with some big boulders in it, but luckily there was no obstruction on the bank except for a sheep fence which I had to climb, and the bank was fairly high so I could keep most of the line clear of the water; so we reached the next pool safely. It was a very rough pool and only a salmon-lie in a much lower water; but the fish stopped in it and played right out in the roughest water. He began tiring after a time and came over to our side of the pool, but there was no easy place from which to gaff him, as there were big stones in a few feet of water right up to the bank. Willie, without a moment's hesitation, was in the freezing water up to the knees wading out to a clear spot beyond the stones. The fish made one more rush into the fast water while Willie crouched, as still as a heron, and waited for him to be brought within his reach. He came slowly into the slacker water, fighting every inch of the way. Willie gaffed him and started wading ashore. The fly fell out of his mouth just as Willie stepped on to the bank with water dripping from his breeches, but we had him, a lovely fish of 17 lbs and covered with sea lice.

In early spring there is usually much rain and melting snow. Rivers are often in flood and coloured, which makes fly fishing impossible, and in the majority of rivers baits are chiefly used early on in the season. Every river has its own usages, but so many more fish are caught per rod on the Tweed than on any other river that they have certainly discovered the best baits for the Tweed, and their conclusions may well apply to a number of other rivers equally well.

On the Tweed natural baits are by far the most widely used. Gold and silver sprats and eel tails, their size varying according to the size and colour of the river, then gold and undyed natural minnows for lower water. These are the staple diet of the Tweed salmon. The argument is that if a fish grips a metal minnow he will feel the unnatural hardness and spit it out again, whereas if he takes a natural minnow, he will hold on until the hooks are pulled in. A boatman on the Tweed will tell you to go on winding in with the reel if a fish is felt, until the line is quite tight, and only then to raise the rod point. It needs a harder pull to hook a fish with a triangle than with a single hook, especially if a fish is holding a bait firmly in his mouth, and a stronger pull can be exerted by reeling the line in than by raising the rod point. If one goes on reeling after the fish has taken the bait in his mouth he will try to turn away with it and so hook himself.

Prawn fishing is a very debatable subject as fish behave in so many different ways when they see a prawn. On the Tweed they are kept until the summer, when the river is full of fish and they will look at nothing else, but on many other rivers they are extensively used early in the season. On the Wye prawns are fished from both banks, every hundred yards, all day and every day from Hereford to the sea. The result is that the majority of fish are caught on prawns and I wouldn't dare to suggest that they are used too much.

To me it is as thrilling to hook a fish on a minnow as on a salmon fly. The first two tugs he gives, which shows it is really a fish, and not the bottom one has hooked, are as exciting as anything in salmon fishing. I remember one ghillie who was describing the finest salmon fisherman he had ever seen, so I asked what bait he preferred to fish with. The ghillie was most indignant and replied that he never fished with anything but a fly. He must have missed a lot of fun and stayed at home on many days when he could have been catching fish if he hadn't been such a purist. For a man to claim that he knows how to fish he should be able to cast a bait as well as a fly, and there is certainly as much in working a bait through the water as in working a fly. I started fishing entirely with a fly and I began bait fishing about twelve years ago, but I don't do enough to be really good and accurate with a bait rod. The good man isn't the one who can fling a bait into the next county, but the man who throws exactly the same length of line at the same angle, each time he casts, and so covers all the water. Some men like to have a piece of cotton tied round the line at about twenty yards from the bait to ensure doing this, when fishing from a boat. For myself I just fish away and hope for the best; but the better man would probably hook more fish.

Generally speaking a bait should be fished fairly slowly as near the bottom as possible without touching it, and it should be over the salmon lie as long as possible; leaving the bait 'hanging' over the lie is often effective. Salmon usually take fairly deep, but I once saw a salmon come right up and take a prawn about 2 ft below the surface when it was being hung over its head by a deaf, red-faced admiral on the Wye. It must have been very near the surface as it broke the surface almost at once, and even the piano wire on which it was probably hooked couldn't have jerked it up from the bottom as quickly as that. The admiral must have been deaf, as after he had landed it he never answered my question as to how large it was.

It is amazing the number of different engines, which may be classed together as baits, that have been devised by human ingenuity to lure salmon; and it is extraordinary when one sees trays and drawers full of them in a London shop that they are all designed to catch the same kind of fish. There are natural baits, sprats, minnows, gudgeon and eel tails mostly dyed the most unnatural colours, yellow, scarlet and even blue, and preserved in chemicals. There are boiled prawns and shrimps, salted, fresh, or preserved, and a hundred different tackles for mounting them on to make them spin, wobble or go straight on through the water. Besides these 'natural' baits there are artificial imitations of fish in metal, wood or celluloid, some resembling fresh-water fish while others are more like a nightmare. There are also many different spoon baits and wagtails, and as if this wasn't a sufficiently wide selection, the most awful-looking 'plug' baits have recently been imported from America. All these baits vary in size from less than one inch to almost six inches in length. I shouldn't be in the least surprised to find a case containing different sizes of hand-grenades one day, as they would certainly be more effective than some of the baits that are displayed.

If one wanted to be 'fully equipped' for spinning for salmon it would cost about £500 and it would need two trunks to carry the baits and tackles alone, and about nine-tenths of the time would be spent in changing lures. After a bit one has one's own preferences. I only fish with about three different baits in a fairly wide range of sizes, but if I am fishing with a ghillie I usually fish with the local favourites, for nothing is worse than a ghillie who has no confidence in one's tackle. Lack of confidence is so very infectious, especially in salmon fishing when there is so much fishing and so little catching. I think it is a good thing to buy baits and tackles from a local shop rather than London, as the ghillie will then know how to handle them and will be quicker in helping to mount baits or change minnows; besides, one can get much useful information from a local fishing-tackle shop. If one has to buy in London it is a good thing to go to the shop with a clear picture of what one wants and a strong determination not to buy anything else. I seldom manage to leave a tackle shop without buying a pound's worth of stuff that I shall probably never use, and I think most other people are the same. It probably pays the shop's rent.

The state of the water and the number of fish in it are much the most important factors in catching spring salmon on baits. The weather also has some effect but chiefly because if it is sufficiently unpleasant few fishermen will torture themselves for long enough to catch many salmon.

I have never fished on the Tweed before the middle of March, but even then it can be bitterly cold, as it was one day when I went to fish the beat just below where the Till enters the Tweed. There had been much rain two nights before and there was a good deal of colour in the Tweed but it looked just fishable. We hoped that the Till might be rather clearer, but what a hope! I stopped and had a look at it as I crossed the bridge, and my heart sank. It was an appalling colour, but as I had come a long way I decided to go on. I found the ghillie waiting for me with a long face. He said it was hopeless and indeed it was below where the Till came in; but the top of the beat was a hundred yards above this.

Just above where the Till enters there is a little island; the main river runs down the far side of it. It was too big and fast to fish in that height of water; but there was a little run between our bank and the island, not more than 30 yards across at the widest and only about 60 yards long, where the stream wasn't too fast. An occasional fish had been caught in it, so we decided to give it a try. We rowed up in the boat, and I put on the largest golden sprat I had; but the river was a terrible colour and it was out of sight when it was about 8 inches under the surface. To add to the improbability of catching a fish it began to snow. I started fishing in the shallow water at the top of the run, without much hope, and I caught the bottom quite often until we reached some rather deeper water, which didn't add to my enjoyment. After a few casts in the deeper water it came on to snow really hard with the wind driving up the river in half a blizzard. I caught the bottom again. I kept pulling at it, and it began to move. I could hardly believe my senses, but I was eventually convinced that I hadn't hooked the handle of an old bucket or any other inanimate object that behaves and feels like a fish, and that I really had hooked a spring salmon. I have never played a fish more carefully, as I was sure it was the only chance I should have and I didn't expect anybody at home to believe me if I said I had lost one. We landed it safely, a clean little fish of 8 lbs and I rejoiced exceedingly.

In very dirty water trout quite often take a golden sprat, and a little fish of about ½ lb chewed up my one from last large golden sprat by flopping about on the surface as I was reeling him in. However, near the bottom of the run I caught another salmon with the remaining one, a fish of 6 lbs. I fished the run down twice more as there was nowhere else to go; but without success, and as I was risking death from exposure every moment I stayed out, I decided to go home after lunch and have a hot bath; but in spite of the weather I had thoroughly enjoyed my morning, as it isn't every day that one catches two fish.

Some wonderful catches of salmon are made on the Tweed in spring and it isn't uncommon for most rods on the lower beats to have double figures in one day. This is quite extraordinary compared with any other salmon fishing I have ever done. I was once able to let my brother know a fortnight beforehand that I was coming on leave and he was lucky enough to be able to take one day on South Wark. It was just a chance as the river might easily have been unfishable. We anxiously watched the weather for some days beforehand; but the great day dawned fine and cold with the water in a fairly reasonable condition although it was rather low for Wark.

It is always interesting to fish a new beat and especially one of the most famous beats on any salmon river in Britain, where catching two or three fish is regarded as a poor day. I started fishing with a golden sprat, but nothing happened so I changed to a silver sprat about 2½ inches long. There were fish showing in every place we fished, which is always most encouraging, and just before lunch I hooked a fish in a fast run behind an island. It would have been a lovely run to fish with a fly and the bait came round almost like one. The fish followed it into comparatively shallow water and took with a swirl and I had him on. He played well in the fast water and took about 15 minutes to land, a clean little fish of 7 lbs. My brother also caught one from the bank and tailed it himself.

After lunch we went downstream and I had the most exciting half-hour I have ever had salmon fishing. At the top of a run and in comparatively shallow water, probably only about three feet deep, there was a swirl made by a large sunken stone. The boatman said there was sometimes a fish behind it. He held the boat just above and to one side, and I threw the bait beyond the swirl and worked it back below the rock. As the bait came into the turbid water behind the rock a fish took it and I had him on. I played him for some time and we had just gone ashore to land him when he got off. We rowed out again and I cast in the same way; the bait came round behind the rock without anything happening, until it was within a few yards of the boat, when I saw the flash of silver as a fish turned and a salmon took with a savage tug. We managed to land this one successfully, a fish of 8 lbs. We rowed out and tried the same spot again. Next cast another fish took; but he was only on for a moment or two. After that they wouldn't play, but I had hooked three salmon in three successive casts, and I don't suppose I shall ever do it again.

I caught three more fish in the afternoon, while my brother caught two from the bank and lost two others, making 8 altogether, all weighing between 6 and 10 lbs. It was a wonderful day and we went home well pleased, as it so seldom happens that a day one is much looking forward to lives up to expectations.

CHAPTER VI

WET FLIES FOR TROUT

I ENJOY downstream wet-fly fishing for trout in the spring, and I look forward to it with renewed anticipation every year. There, I have said it—a rank heresy has been written in plain black on a plain white sheet of paper.

Wet-fly fishing comes in for more abuse than any other kind of fishing. The dry-fly fisherman who often writes more thousands of words than he catches fish is the worst offender. He mistakenly thinks that his form of fishing is the only artistic and decent way of catching a trout. The Untouchables in India couldn't be more scorned by the Touchables than the wet-fly fisher is by the dry-fly man, or purist, as he pleases to call himself. He sneeringly calls wet-fly fishing the 'chuck and chance it' method, as though he had some form of divine control over the fish he cast for and left nothing to chance. I also resent the word 'chuck'. It should be kept for describing what the squire does to the milkmaid 'neath the chin. This attitude is like the man who rides in the show-ring affecting to despise the man who goes out hunting. Every fisherman goes out fishing to catch fish, and however much he may like to hear the willow-warblers warbling in the willows, they are a pretty poor compensation for a series of blank days' fishing.

In some streams dry-flies are used because this is the best way of catching trout and does least to disturb water over which a number of people want to fish. On other waters where the rivers are bigger and faster and there are more fish per fisherman, wet-flies are used, when this is the best method of catching a good basketful of trouts. Although the purist will be loth to believe it, there is a high degree of skill required in catching a trout fishing downstream with a wet-fly, and the actual strike is usually more difficult than anything the dry-fly man is called upon to perform. There should be far more good-will and toler-

The Eden (Westmorland)

ance among fishermen, for we all go fishing for our pleasure, and a charitable attitude is the best for approaching either a river bank or a blank sheet of foolscap.

I started fishing in Westmorland in the Easter holidays when I was quite young. I used to look forward to it towards the end of the winter, until April came with its bright days and the first pale green on the larches and the birds making the dawn-light loud with their song. Rods and waders had to be taken out and inspected, and my father used to tie flies beforehand, with a small inquisitive boy leaning over the table and keeping awfully quiet and still when the silk broke or things weren't going too well. He used to tie them without a vice, holding a No. 1 or No. 2 hook in his left hand and using his right hand to tie in the silks, dubbing and feathers. It isn't very easy to tie small flies without a vice to hold the hooks. It allows too much opportunity for silks and feathers to slip or break at a critical moment. Things used not always to go too smoothly, but he would produce quite a few waterhen, red partridge and light snipe and purple, which would be augmented later by purchases from Wilkinson's in Penrith.

We motored over from Yorkshire, sometimes for the day, but more usually we stayed for a week at Edenhall in an extremely comfortable hotel where we have been ever since. The drive over Bowes Moor was the beginning of the adventure; a strip of unfenced tarmac stretching across the open moor with tall stones along the verges to show its whereabouts, when snow lies deep. We would stop on the summit and listen to the cock-grouse calling from the hummocks and the whistle of golden plover, while my father smoked a cigarette. The Lakeland hills could be seen, their jagged peaks standing out a deep blue against the pale of the sky. From here the road descends to Brough and Appleby, which I always liked because my father used to call it Applepie. We would look at all the little streams by the roadside on the way down to the Eden Valley, to see how much water they had in them, but it was at Appleby that we had our first glimpse of the Eden and could see what sort of fishing-order it was in and make our final plans where to go.

There was one more stop at Temple Sowerby where we bought licences from the Post Office, and by judicious staring in the right direction I would be presented with a large slab of chocolate. A Roman road runs from here to Penrith, but we usually turned off half-way along it and took the road to the Udford ford. This soon became a grassy lane with little rabbits rushing across it and into holes in the stone walls, and bright cock pheasants jumping up and standing for a moment on top of the wall before disappearing into the plantations beyond. The car was stopped just above the little bank where the track dipped down into the river. There was a plantation on the left, and on the right open fields stretching across to the junction of the Eden and Eamont; beyond rose woods and fields, and in the distance Cross Fell with a patch of snow on the summit. As the noise of the engine stopped, the sound of water flowing over shallows could be heard and the call of plover and the spring note of the curlew as they rose from the rushy field beside the track.

Rods and waders would be taken out and dealt with and eventually everything would be ready. Soon clear running water would drive the air from my waders and press the cold canvas against my legs as I waded out into the top of a stream to begin fishing. The feeling of suppressed excitement at the beginning of the first day's fishing of the season is the same today as it was then.

The Eamont at Udford is one of the loveliest stretches of water I know. It flows between red sandstone cliffs and wooded banks, with grass fields running down to the river in places. The river is a series of fast runs and pools; the water, white and broken in places, but smooth enough in the pools to reflect the colours of the banks. The sound of running water is always in the air, with the song of birds and the call of woodpigeons superimposed.

My father was very fond of a run just below the ford, called the 'stumps', where the river runs out of the woods and between flat grass fields. He made me fish it down first and he used to follow some way behind and fish the water beyond where I could reach. There is an island near the shore and we used to wade across to this and from there out into the main river beyond. Trees grew on the island overhanging the water and I couldn't wade quite far enough out to avoid the risk of catching them, so I had to use a short line at first, but as I waded further down the run I let out more line. The flies fell into the fast rippling water and came round with the stream until they lay below me, when I would cast again. Sometimes the rod point would dip, and if I was lucky a fat speckled brown trout would be wriggling on the end of the cast, sending the first thrill of playing a fish along the tight line and down my little split-cane rod. I never caught very many when I first started, as I usually struck far too hard and left hundreds of flies embedded in the mouths of unfortunate fish, but I was terribly keen and used to be on the go all day until my legs ached from walking in waders.

When it was time to go home I would reluctantly return to the car, already making plans for the next day and with the comforting thought that only one day had gone.

My younger brother Mark soon began fishing, and recently we have spent many holidays together fishing the Yorkshire Anglers' water on the Eden and Eamont. We still spent the days in much the same way as we used to as boys. The piece of water to be fished had to be decided at breakfast, and sometimes we fished together, but more usually we went to different places as we each had our pet spots. He was very fond of the water above Udford at Honey Pot Farm, and I usually preferred the wider water of the Eden below the meeting of the waters where the Eamont joins it, but much used to depend on the direction and strength of the wind. It is no use starting fishing too early at the beginning of April, and after breakfast we usually drove into Penrith, about three miles away, to replenish our flies and casts from Wilkinson's tackle shop. We would also visit the baker's, full of the lovely smell of baking bread, and buy cakes and jam puffs hot from the oven before we went our separate ways down to the river.

There is much controversy among wet-fly fishermen as to whether the trout should be approached from above or below, and the upstream fisherman is apt to become rather dogmatic about it and regard his brother the downstream fisher with scorn; he is also more apt to go into print, so one seldom sees any support for fishing downstream, but there is much to be said for both methods.

I started fishing downstream as my father taught me this way, and it is much easier for the beginner whose line may not fall very straight on the water, since the current soon straightens it out and works the fly round without any assistance from the angler. Another advantage is that more water can be covered thoroughly with far fewer casts than are needed upstream. The flies fished across and downstream work in an arc round the fisherman and he covers the water as a man with a scythe covers a field. This is a definite advantage on broad fast rivers when few fish are thinking of rising, as the larger the area that is covered the greater is the chance of the flies passing over a rising fish. The man fishing upstream must work much harder, as his flies float straight back down the stream. If the current is strong they can only be left in the water for a few seconds before he has to cast again. It may also need ten or more casts to cover the same width of water as will be covered by one cast fished downstream. The advantages of upstream fishing are that a shorter line is needed; the flies probably appear more natural in the water on the whole and the chances of hooking a fish that is risen are much better. This method is usually superior on small clear rivers and when fish can be seen rising or bulging.

Soon after I began I used occasionally to fish upstream. After I caught a good basket one day and read some literature on the subject, I went over to the 'upstream' camp completely, and even slightly despised people who fished downstream, until I learnt my lesson. There is a very good run on the Eden just below the village of Langwathby. It is over 200 yards long, with shingle on the near side and mossy rocks in about four feet of water beyond. It is full of fish and one day in April I went there and started fishing at the bottom of the run. The first martins were skimming the surface of the river which showed that flies were hatching out, and I caught a fish almost at once in the glide at the tail of the pool. He fought like a tiger, flashing brown and white in the clear fast water; he was 12 inches long and in good condition. I worked my way upstream a step at a time, casting up and across so that the flies drifted down over the rocks and holes on the far side of the stream. For each step forward I made several different casts at varying angles to cover the whole of the water within reach. A trout quite often rose to a natural fly within my reach, and I caught three that I had seen rising in quick succession from a fast little run near my bank. I had caught thirteen by lunch time, all over 10 inches and mostly 12 inches to 14 inches long, and as I looked like reaching my limit of twenty quite easily I sat down to my lunch in a contented frame of mind, without the feeling that I might be missing the rise, which so often seems to coincide with lunch.

When I had finished my sandwiches and smoked a pipe I started again at the bottom and began to fish up in the same way. I couldn't see any trout rising now but there were still a few martins about and I never doubted that I should catch some. I fished for an hour from 1.30 to 2.30, usually the best part of the day, without a touch, although I covered all the best spots in the stream. At last in desperation I began fishing downstream from the top, but with absolutely no confidence, as there was no reason I could see why the fish should take a fly fished downstream any better—but they did, and I caught three in a quarter of an hour. I thought they had probably come on to rise so I started fishing upstream again, but still with equally little success, and after a while I gave it up for good. As soon as I began fishing down again I went on catching fish, and within half an hour I had the remaining four, which gave me twenty altogether.

I couldn't explain it then and I still can't to-day, unless the nymphs looked more natural when they were being fished downstream and pulled against the current. Do nymphs swim gently against the stream when they are coming to the surface? I think they must or trout would never take a nymph fished downstream. A fish will seldom take a dry-fly that is being dragged upstream along the surface, as the natural insect doesn't do this, and even a wild North-Country trout isn't such a fool as to take a fly behaving quite unlike anything it has ever seen before. On one occasion I caught a good trout on a chalk stream, fishing a nymph over it downstream and moving it in little jerks past his nose, when he simply wouldn't look at the same nymph fished from below floating past him with the stream. This encourages me in the belief that nymphs have an active motion through the water on their way to the surface.

I now combine both methods and fish upstream or downstream, depending on the conditions. I believe this is the most sensible attitude to adopt provided one isn't interfering with anyone else's sport by putting down an undue number of fish.

Wet-flies are imitations of the nymph stage of the fly. They hatch on the bottom of the river, where the eggs sink after they are laid, and come to the surface to dry before flying away in their adult stage. It takes the fly several seconds, depending on the atmosphere, before its wings are dry enough for it to fly, and fish take them on their way to the surface and while they are resting on top of it.

There is probably more conservatism over the types of wet-flies that are used than over any other kind of fishing tackle. The same flies are used to-day as were used many years ago. The hackles are of English birds, partridge, snipe and woodcock, and the bodies are of water-rat or mole fur, or hare's ear or plain coloured silk. They are simple flies and very often the more bare the hook becomes the better the fish like it. The hackles represent the miniature wings and legs of the nymph and six fairly short strands are sufficient. After one has caught half a dozen trout on the same fly the hook is usually almost naked, and it looks so bare that nobody would ever dream of buying or trying a fly like it, but the fish still rise to it and even take it more readily than a heavily dressed fly. I had a 'Greenwell's Glory' in the lapel of a tweed coat when I first met my wife and I was never allowed to remove it. I wore the coat every time I put on civilian clothes for a year, and as it was a fly I had made myself it didn't stand the strain too well. The wing and most of the hackle came off until only three strands were left, but I caught a trout on it last spring. I sometimes wonder the fish doesn't see the hook and become scared, but I suppose the reason is that the fly rests in the water with the hook vertically below the shank and as the fish usually approaches and takes from below it doesn't see the full horror of what is in store for it.

The best size of fly for all waters is a No. 2, but I find a No. 3 better in very big waters and I add a bit of tinsel to the body. In low water a No. 1 hook may be better. 3x points are sufficiently light for most occasions, although 4x is better in very low clear water. I usually fish with three flies equally spaced up the cast.

Spring fishing is much affected by weather and water. When I was young I used to think that a big water must be a disadvantage as it would spread the fish out over too large an area, but this isn't the case. A flood at the beginning of a holiday is the best thing that can happen, even if the water becomes too coloured and stops fishing for a day. Trout will take in a rising water until it becomes too coloured, and even when it is filthy one may find an odd trout still taking flies that have drifted into a backwater. I found a fish doing this on the Eamont one day when I was walking back to the car, as the river had suddenly come down a rich chocolate colour. He was in quite shallow water and he took a wet-fly as soon as it fell over him. He must have been quite a big fish as he rushed out into the stream tearing the line from the rod, but unfortunately he came off almost at once.

A big water when the stain of mud has left it and it still looks black is the best for wet-fly fishing. There is far more water to fish when rivers are big than when they are low. The fish spread out and there seem to be plenty everywhere. In the olden days the rivers used to stay in this condition for days, as field draining was less well done and the ground held the water for longer after it had rained. The local landowners only bothered to fish under these conditions and they often caught forty or fifty trout in a day. Nowadays rivers run in much more rapidly and are seldom in perfect condition for more than two or three days after a flood.

It is still possible to catch a great many trout under these conditions. The Yorkshire Anglers have wisely made a limit of twenty trout for any rod on any one day, as even on Association water which is fairly heavily fished it is quite often possible to catch more than this number in April, but ten brace should be enough for any man.

With a big water, weather conditions matter much less than low water, and fish take in snow showers or bright sunshine nearly as well as under conditions more usually associated with fish rising. My father told me that during the best week he ever had with some friends, they woke up to find 3 inches of snow on the ground every morning. It melted during the day and was sufficient to keep the river up and the fish took well every day. The weather at the beginning of April can be very variable: one day it is as mild as summer with a sun so hot that one has to fish in shirt sleeves for comfort, while the next the 'Helm' wind comes howling over the snow-covered Pennines and blows flurries of sleet up the river into the faces of shivering anglers.

A wind is sometimes useful for fishing flat and otherwise calm stretches of the river. There is a broad pool in the Eden called the 'Carnatic' which has large patches of green weed on the bottom, especially near the tail of the pool. Fish seem to like them, and it holds a great many very good trout. A North East wind strikes up and across it and the glide at the tail fishes very well from the right bank under these conditions. There was a strong North-East wind and not a cloud in the sky one April day, so I decided to go and fish there as it seemed the best chance. As I walked down from the farm where I left the car, the river stretched out below me sparkling blue among the green fields, with darker woods rising beyond and the lakeland mountains pale in the distance. Oyster catchers and redshanks rose from the shingle as I approached the river and added their cries to the sound of water. It was quite warm in the sun and I took off my coat and fished in high waders and shirtsleeves, starting at the bottom of the glide and working my way upstream; the flies cast up and across came bobbing down on the little waves which the wind made by blowing against the current.

The trout seemed delighted with the way they worked. There were quite a few fish rising to the natural flies and they took mine very well. I only fished a stretch about sixty yards long, keeping near the bank the first time I fished it up and wading a little further out each successive time until the water became too deep.

There is a rough stream just below, which I fished to give the Carnatic a rest. The stream was rather too strong for upstream fishing and the fish took a fly fished downstream very well, but the slight bow in the line from an upstream wind made striking rather difficult. I had caught twenty fish by 2.30 p.m. after only fishing for about four hours. They were a very good average size, weighing 15 lbs between them. Mark was fishing further up near the meeting of the waters and he caught eighteen on the same day.

The fishing is not always as good as this. A hard frost at night does as much harm as anything else. We reckoned that when it froze the night before it reduced one's catch by about half. On some days when the water was very low and it froze at night it needed hard work to catch more than two or three fish a day. Then it seemed impossible that it was ever easy to catch as many as one wanted. It isn't easy to explain this, but probably a thin coat of ice is formed over the stones in shallow water, as they radiate heat more quickly than the water, and this makes the water in contact freeze. A frost would also probably kill some of the flies that had already hatched and were waiting to return to the water to lay their eggs. Generally speaking we caught more fish from the Eden than the Eamont. I only once caught my limit in the Eamont. We never kept trout under 10 inches and we reckoned that six from the Eamont and ten from the Eden was an average day, any more was good and any less was poor, but I often averaged ten a day over the whole holiday.

Towards the end of April and the beginning of May the fishing often goes off as the trout are distracted from taking ordinary flies by creepers, stone flies and clouds of awful 'gran-nom', evil-tasting flies which hatch in millions and cover the surface of the water. The trout take one or two but they can't taste very nice as they soon stop taking and will look at nothing else.

There is a feeling of lightness and freedom when one takes off one's waders after a day's fishing, and how good is tea! Hot buttered toast and scones and strawberry jam, with plenty of cakes, sitting in an armchair in front of the fire, then a pipe afterwards while discussing events of interest which occurred during the day's fishing. When one knows the water it is almost like having another day's fishing to hear the description of a friend's day.

After tea we used to go out together with one rod between us, and spend part of the evening in looking for plover's eggs on the red ploughed fields down by the river. When we found a nest we furtively secreted the eggs in our pockets and took them back to the hotel to be served as a savoury at a later date. We never bothered with waders after tea, but looked for trout near the bank taking flies that had drifted out of the current and into backwater during the day, or spent flies that returned to lay their eggs. We usually fished with a dry-fly and there were often trout rising in the boat pool at Udford, where the river was sheltered from the wind by the high wooded bank opposite the farm where we left the car. There were often good trout in the shallow water under the trees and sometimes they swam in a shoal, not unlike dace, and just dimpled the surface out in the middle of the pool. We could see them in the water and they took a dry-fly quite well, but they lay well out and were difficult to strike on a long line. It was very pleasant down by the river on a warm evening with the sun low in the sky. The shadows of the trees stretched across the water and fields, and the birds sang their evening songs. As it became dark the drumming of snipe could be heard and a woodcock would fly up the river making its own little sounds in the soft twilight.

CHAPTER VII

WARTIME FISHING FOR TROUT

WHEN I was living a fairly hectic life and putting in many flying hours without very much time off, every moment away from the war effort was welcome. I always found fishing was the best form of relaxation from anything connected with aeroplanes, and after an evening's fishing I used to feel quite different.

When we were flying from a relief landing-ground my wife used sometimes to drive out and pick me up after we finished flying. I looked forward to it all day. Sometimes I would find I was rather a long way from the landing-ground when it was nearly time to stop flying. Down would go the nose and the machine would be surprised by the speed at which it returned to its roost.

I had permission to fish a lovely stretch of the Leach, which is a crystal-clear stream running off the Cotswolds and into the Thames at Lechlade. People are especially kind in allowing men in the Forces to fish and I had many delightful days here and elsewhere. The stream runs through a very small Cotswold village, with a mill just above the road bridge. The water from the mill runs alongside the road for about sixty yards and empties into the main river in a pool just above the bridge. We used to leave the car under a huge chestnut tree by the roadside. After I had put the rod up we took our picnic basket back to the bridge and sat on the wall while we ate our tea; what a tea it used to be! Always three kinds of sandwiches, cheese and tomato, egg, and jam, and home-made cake, either sponge or chocolate, and shortbread—I only wish I had a tea like that in front of me now. The R.A.F. bus generally passed us while we were eating, with a wave of hands and a swirl of dust. Then we had the place to ourselves again except for the sleek redpoll cattle in the field beyond the pool. There were two big fish in the pool, and sometimes one would rise in the middle of tea:

most inconsiderate, as it caused an interruption if it seemed in a likely place, but the fly usually dragged before it reached them and tea was continued in peace. But one day one made a mistake and was held up in triumph as the bus went by just to show that I sometimes did catch a fish.

After tea it would be warm in the evening sunshine and when the tea-things had been put away we would wander downstream a short way, first through our host's garden, which ran down to the river and was sweet with the scent of many roses and bright with flowers and rippling water; and then through fields along the row of willows which overhung the stream.

The river is very small, but it compares most favourably with any other of its size in the South of England. It was so full of fish that it was almost impossible not to send a fish streaking upstream whenever one approached it, and so disturb any fish rising in the stretch above, but I generally managed to catch a trout after tea. A fish of a pound was a good one, but I never kept anything under 11 inches and they were always as fat as little pigs and played amazingly well for South-Country trout. We used to work our way upstream again after an hour or so, but instead of following the river through the village we followed the road to the 'Swan', where there was always a great welcome awaiting us. We had to go into the kitchen and sit down, while Albert drew us glasses of beer and Mrs Newman told us all the local news.

When the light began to fail we went out above the mill. I used to cast a slightly inaccurate fly on to a deep stretch of water which was fairly clear of trees and held some large trout. There was one in particular that must have been nearly 2 lbs, just above a weed rack. I am sure if he had been hooked he would have shot straight through it, but although I rose him once or twice I never managed to hook him. There were generally a lot of fish rising when the air began to cool and the spent gnats came down, but I usually had difficulty in getting them to take an artificial fly, and a brace of trout was quite a good evening. When they stopped rising we drove back in the growing darkness, with warmth striking up from the road and

The Wiltshire Avon

the cooler evening air fresh in our faces, to a hot supper at home and the prospect of fried trout for breakfast. It is good to think of it now, with snow on the ground outside and beyond it barbed wire guarded by machine guns.

Some big trout used to work their way up the little stream from the pool above the bridge to the mill, when the may-fly were up. The trouble was if one looked over the wall the fish saw one and was off, and if one didn't one couldn't see the fish. We thought of a plan of campaign. Jane stood well downstream where she could see, while I dangled the fly over the wall, and she directed the fly over the fish and shouted when I was to strike. It was very exciting but not terribly effective!

A number of fish lived at the top of the little stream where it emerged from a culvert after working the mill. They came out into the shallow water just below to feed, but as soon as a head appeared over the wall a little one would go shooting upstream, spreading alarm and despondency among the rest, and the whole flock would take cover in the culvert. The larger fish were sometimes rather braver and didn't make a bolt for it, but a certain quickening of their swimming showed that they were on the alert and in no mood to take a fly. These fish led a pretty disturbed life, as village children never passed without looking over the wall, and I should have thought they would have become used to faces looking at them, but they never seemed to. Occasionally by great stealth one could spot a fish feeding without disturbing any others, but the fishing wasn't very easy as there was a telephone wire at exactly the right height and distance behind for the fly to catch on and almost invariably a small fish below the one selected would be disturbed by the line landing on the water. There were some good fish there, and they still are as far as I am concerned, as I only managed to catch one keepable fish out of all the times I fished it.

The trout in the deep water above the mill were difficult in daytime as they were very critical and the water floated the fly over them so slowly that they had plenty of time to have a good look at it. I have often found that in water of this kind a fish is more likely to take if he is close up against the bank, especially if one can make the fly hit the bank and bounce off on to the water. An iron-blue cocked well up on the water sometimes lured these fish against their finer judgement, but even when they were hooked they stood a good chance of getting off as they played so strongly and there was quite a lot of weed about. It usually needed two 4x points on the end of the cast to give one a chance of rising these fish.

The first fish I caught on the Leach was near the top of this deep stretch. It was a fairly cold day early in May and very few fish were moving, but I found one rising regularly opposite a stump where a tree had fallen across the river. The light was wrong so I couldn't see him in the water, but he made quite a good rise. He was lying just where the water flowed a little faster as it passed the stump. It was a good 'iron-blue' day and sure enough he took it the first time it came over him. As soon as he felt the hook he went off with a terrific rush, which it was impossible to stop with a 4x cast, but I held him as hard as I dared and after a few minutes he came back to me and I landed him. He was only 12 inches long but he weighed 14 ozs. I went on upstream and as I passed the place where he had been lying I realised how lucky I had been to land him. Below the surface the river was full of the leafless branches of the fallen tree, among which he had rushed as soon as he was hooked, but by a lucky chance he had come out the same way that he went in.

The fishing ended at the top of this stretch where the water emerged from beneath a stone foot-bridge with three arches. A trout of over a pound lived under the far arch, but he confined most of his feeding activities to the inside of the bridge; only the end of a ring would float out to show he was rising, but sometimes he would drop down and take a fly just below the bridge. I spent a lot of time waiting for him to come out, as a fly which hit against the bridge and landed on his nose should have been irresistible, but I never caught him, as when he did appear I never managed to land the fly on the right spot although I could do it every time when he was under the bridge.

Below the mill the river was all fast water and shallow pools with nicely spaced weed patches. There were a lot of trees, which made it difficult fishing, but if one could get a fly over a rising fish he would often have it, as he had such a short time in which to criticize the fly, and I always find it much easier to strike a fish in fast shallow water. One day I found a fish rising very regularly in this fast water. As he was in a fairly easy place to fish he looked a certainty. For once my fly landed just right and floated cocked up on the water about three inches to his left, but he didn't even turn towards it. He went on taking the natural fly but he wouldn't look at mine while it floated past to his left. Then one cast landed just to his right and he took it at once. I couldn't understand it until I landed him and found he was blind in the left eye.

There was one pool just below the garden which had a strand of barbed wire across the bottom to stop cattle from wandering upstream into the garden, and there were several good fish in it, but it meant casting over the wire. Part of the line rested on the wire while the rest lay on the water beyond. The fish were fairly unsuspicious and I rose quite a few, but they were difficult to strike over the wire, and had a way of running back under it or diving under a tree-trunk which hung out over the water when they were hooked. It always meant getting one's feet wet to land them; but I caught quite a few fat trout from that pool.

Trout used to live in the very thinnest water sometimes with their backs barely covered. There was a tiny backwater with only a few inches of fast running water covering the gravel, which held some remarkably good fish. They were all lovely light-coloured fish and very difficult to see against the gravel before they saw you; but Jane was very good at spotting them. I caught several good trout from here, the biggest being over a pound, and he can't have been in more than 5 inches of water.

There was another even smaller stream near the main aerodrome where we often went when I was flying from there, as it was so close at hand, but unfortunately the Thames Conservancy had been dredging the year before and had practically ruined it for the time. There were plenty of small fish about, and all were in excellent condition, which augured well for the future. Before the purge my host told me there had been fish up to 2lbs, but when I was there very few fish were takeable. I hope in a few years' time that it will be as good as formerly, and that he will catch many more big fish out of it. It was very pleasant down by the stream in the evening. Although it ran within a few fields of the aerodrome one was completely shut off from it and might have been in another world.

I have always had a great notion to see fish in the water from different places and under different conditions. I have often seen them from a car, although it doesn't count if one stops the car, and once or twice I have seen fish in a river from a train. I thought it might be just possible to see them from the air. When I was stationed near the Hampshire Avon, I used to fly up and down as low and as slowly as possible and try to pick up fish in the water. After I had narrowly missed a few trees and telegraph wires I went up with another man and made him fly the machine while I hung my head out over the side and looked for the fish. I had to wear goggles for this, which made it rather more difficult to see and I never actually picked one up. The trouble is that one can't keep one's eye on a spot for quite long enough before one has to transfer one's gaze to a place at least a hundred yards away; but I am sure it could be done if one knew exactly where a large fish lay over a light patch of weeds, as every weed bed shows up very clearly and a fish should be silhouetted against the light green.

I thought it might be easier to see a salmon so I tried once or twice over the Wye in Wales, but I had to keep higher as the country is so much more hilly and I was equally unsuccessful there. I saw a man playing a fish on the Usk one day and I flew around to see how he was getting on but the hills rather got in the way.

Besides flying I always used to look for birds and farm from the air. During harvest I could give an account of how it was getting on for several counties round where I was stationed. As we approached the coast just before the German *flak* made such excellent shooting at us, I saw a little flock of widgeon fly away. At the same time as I was looking for fish from the air, I used a plane to see how weed-cutting was going on. There were

Rooksbury Mill Pool on the Anton (Hampshire)

two or three stretches on the river Avon where I had permission to fish and I chose the best place by aerial survey before setting out in the evening to fish, petrol for a car being so very precious.

I had only one day on the Avon last Summer but I was lucky to get a 48-hour leave at the same time as my host and we had a delightful day together. Although the fishing wasn't very good, my wife and I used this as an excuse to spend much of the time in the garden where there was a wonderful crop of cherries and lots of strawberries and a few gooseberries and raspberries. We made real pigs of ourselves and took pockets full of cherries to eat as we fished. We did outwit one nice trout which was taking nymphs, although our nymph fishing wasn't the skilful scientific affair of some fishermen. We knew the fish was nymphing but we had no idea what nymph it was taking, so A. tied a series of nymphs on to our two rods alternately while I did the fishing. He was a good loader and eventually the fish, surprised by the immense variety of nymphs coming over him, took mine. For once I struck right and had him. It was a lovely sunny day and we all enjoyed ourselves, as it is so seldom that two leaves coincide and one sees friends in wartime.

We went for one or two 48-hour leaves to stay with my uncle near Andover, and fish on the Anton, but the Anton is generally rather disappointing. It is full of fish, many of them are a good size, but they spend all their time with their heads buried in weed patches and their tails waving in the air looking for shrimps or some other aquatic bug. They take their heads out for a few seconds to munch what they have caught and then put them back in again. It needs a terrific hatch of flies to take their minds off their infernal shrimps and induce them to rise properly. Lately I have been unlucky in hitting off a good rise. Very few of these tailing fish will look at a nymph, but if the fish is moving about over a patch of weeds and only occasionally burrowing into it he may take a nymph as he is probably on the look-out for one between his mouthfuls of weed. If he is stationary over a weed bed and continually sticking his head into it he is a waste of time whatever anybody says. The only way to catch him is to stalk up behind and catch him with a landing-net when he isn't looking. I have read so much about the ease with which these fish can be caught with a nymph that I have been induced to waste hours trying to catch them, but I am not going to waste any more time and I strongly advise anybody else not to do so either. Perhaps the fishermen who keep saying how easy these fish are to catch want to keep their fellow anglers harmlessly occupied while they catch the easier fish.

The fish above Rooksbury Mill behave much better and are far more free-rising, although the water is deeper and slower and one would expect them to rise less readily. The reason for this is that my uncle has from time to time put quite a lot of fish in above the mill, and new fish undoubtedly take better than the old indigenous fish. I did once catch a beautiful fat trout of 2 lbs below the mill on a dry fly. Although he was lying where the town sewer enters the river he had firm pink flesh and was wonderful good eating, but the majority of trout from the Anton and Hampshire Avon aren't very good to eat. My uncle's house is delightfully situated just by the mill, which is no longer worked, and surrounded by the gentle sound of water. One little stream runs out from under the drawing-room window. There is usually a trout in it, which I have often tried for from the drawing-room, but so far without success. There is hardly a window in the house from which one can't see a trout, which is a pity in a way as I am usually late for dinner as a result.

I had a great idea for poaching innumerable fish out of the South-Country chalk streams, and I still believe it would work if one had plenty of petrol and could try it, although one might end up behind the bars. I think I shall have had enough of prison life by the end of this war to last me a lifetime. If one stops on any bridge over the Avon, Kennet or Test and probably any other chalk stream, and looks over the parapet, there are always huge fish lazily swimming about. If the bridge is anywhere near human habitation these fish will probably know all about bread already. Even if they don't they need little education. The scheme was to buy a few loaves of bread and educate a number of fish below a lot of different bridges in the same neighbourhood; quite a harmless occupation for a Sunday afternoon, and nobody would have the least suspicion that a foul deed of poaching was contemplated. The next morning at crack of dawn the fish would again find bits of bread floating over them, but this time after a preliminary hors-d'œuvre a hook would be concealed in the bread, and the unsuspecting fish would very soon find themselves on the bank. I was fully prepared to carry out this dastardly crime on an enormous trout which lives in the middle of Hungerford and is fed on bread by all the worthy citizens. The tackle was ready in the car, complete with loaf of bread, sea trout cast and bare hook, and I even left a dance early with an accomplice so that we should be there as soon as possible after it was light enough to start operations. We had it all buttoned up: first the fish was to be put well on the rise by a liberal hatch of bread, then the hook would be lowered down embedded in a juicy piece of crust. The striking was to be done by hand and the fish played and landed from somebody's garden just beside the road. There wasn't a soul in sight, but unfortunately the fish wasn't either, although when the rest of the party came home a little later he had appeared. I should especially like to catch some of the enormous semi-tame fish which are kept as pets and fed on bread every morning after breakfast; although one couldn't be present to see the faces of their proud masters when they arrived to find them gone.

There is a hatch-house on the Avon which has a large pool below it and is an excellent place for shady tactics. The only means of entrance is through a hole in the roof as the door is kept locked, but once inside one is out of sight. The house is built on concrete slabs about 4 feet apart, between which the water flows, and there are big cracks between the floor boards. The first thing to do is to spot a fish in one of these streams and induce it to take bread by dropping the remains of one's sandwiches from lunch through the cracks in the floor. The concrete slabs protrude slightly beyond the house into the pool below and a fly has to be cast from the bank so that it lands on the correct one. Then a stealthy hand appears and the fly and cast disappear into the house. The man on the bank just waits and tries to look innocent, but inside the house is great activity. The fly is embedded in bread and lowered into the water in front of the fish by the accomplice, who is lying on his tummy with his eye to the widest crack. It is difficult to see what is happening but the fish quite often takes the fatal piece of bread. The man in the house strikes when he feels anything and lets go with a terrific yell. The fish shoots out into the pool and is played and landed by the man on the bank. Hardly an orthodox way of catching fish, perhaps; but it took a lot of working out and is a most amusing way of spending an hour when the fish aren't rising.

People are so kind about giving permission to fish in wartime that it is a great mistake to poach, however exciting it may be, but one day the temptation was too great for me. I had driven up to Oxfordshire to see my wife when we were engaged and we went for a picnic in the Cotswolds. We had lunch by a tiny stream and after lunch we went for a walk. There were a few little fish in the river, which was quite minute, but in one corner to my amazement we found quite a nice one rising. We were miles from anywhere and I had my rod in the car—I just couldn't resist the temptation. He took the fly like a lamb, but there was some soft ground and rushes between myself and the fish, and I had to run round as soon as I hooked him and pull him downstream from below before I could land him. He was a fat little fish, 12 inches long, and I was told that he was very good for breakfast the next morning.

CHAPTER VIII

FISHING ABROAD

I USED to visit Southern Germany, little thinking that on my next visit I should be accompanied from Holland by four large fully armed soldiers, who although they were quite nice about it, made it quite clear that they would fill me full of holes if I tried to leave them.

I went to Germany first in 1930 with the intention of learning German before I went to Cambridge. I stayed with a family in Munich, and it wasn't long before I began looking round for some fishing, as I was fully equipped with riding breeches in case I met a horse, and fishing-rods in case there might be any fishing. There was a good fishing-tackle shop appropriately called 'Stork', which I used to visit, and they told me of various places where one could fish; one was at Oberau, where the Hotel Gasthof Post had fishing for the guests, but first I had to have a fishing licence.

On a fine spring morning I went to the enormous police building in Ett Strasse, where I showed my passport many times and was eventually admitted to the correct department, where I waited in a queue until it was my turn to speak through the little window in the wall to the official in the office behind. I told him what I wanted in my best German. At first he said it was impossible, no foreigner ever had fished in Germany or ever would as far as he was concerned. I knew this was nonsense, so I persisted and eventually after great consultations with the rest of the men in the office an older man came forward and looked at my passport. He read it from cover to cover and eventually said in triumph that I was under 21, so it was impossible for me to have a fishing licence unless I had written permission from my father, countersigned by a German vice-Consul in England. He thought he had me at last and visions of fishing in Germany were fast receding in my mind, as I thought it very unlikely that I ever should get a licence. I wrote to my father explaining the situation and the wonderful man sent me the necessary letter by return of post. He had found a genuine vice-consul, in Middlesbro' of all unlikely places to look for one.

I took the letter and a photograph in triumph to the police station. The man was so surprised that he gave me the licence, or Fischer Karte, without any further argument, and even gave it me at the reduced price of 12 R.M. instead of 30 R.M. as I was a 'Student'. The whole business so impressed itself on his memory that whenever I went back in after years he greeted me as an old friend, and said he supposed that I was still a 'Student'. He may have been impressed because I was the only man ever to get the necessary permission from England. Two of my friends went to get licences subsequently. Each time the man explained what they must do and said to an underling 'Just fetch me one of those letters from England, will you?' and each time my letter was produced. They both eventually got licences by other methods, one by saying that his father was dead, and that he would write to Goering unless he was given one immediately.

The *Fischer Karte* was a wonderful affair of green cardboard, with my photograph and description on one side and a list of fish and when they were in season and the minimum size they must be, on the other. One also had to have the written permission of the owner of the fishing.

They had to be produced on demand of various green-coated policemen, who prowled about the rivers and suddenly materialised when one was fishing a run. The most important one at Oberau carried a sword and a pistol and had a little beard which seemed to absorb some of the colour of his uniform, so he was always known as 'the man with the green beard'. The second in command just carried a pistol, while the third and last was unarmed and seemed to feel his inferiority keenly.

Oberau is a little Bavarian village about six miles north of Garmisch Partenkirchen. We went over there by train from Munich from the Starnberger Bahnhof. The journey took about 1½ hours in express train and for the last half of the journey the Bavarian Alps were clearly visible, at first as snow-covered

A baby roedeer (Bavaria)

The Lauderbach (Bavaria)

mountains in the distance, and finally close at hand. The river Loisach runs from a ridge of high mountains, the Wetterstein Gebirge, beyond Garmisch, through a valley in the foothills and out into the Bavarian lowlands at Murnau. The bottom of the valley is about a mile wide and very flat, and pine-clad mountains rise precipitously from it. The road and railway run along the valley and in places the river comes close to the line. We always used to look out anxiously to see whether the river was in good order for fishing.

The train only stopped at Oberau for about one minute so we had to be ready to get off the moment it stopped, with rods and kit-bags stacked in the corridor. The train would be out of sight before we had collected our belongings and taken them to the little station, where swallows used to nest on the lamps and in the ticket office; sheets of newspaper were spread on the ground below their nests to keep it clean. Just outside the station and across a gravel road was the Hotel, with green creepers growing up the walls and flowers in the window-boxes. It was spotlessly clean and very comfortable. The cooking was first class; one could get a hot meal from an enormous à la carte menu from 11 a.m. until 11 p.m. and it didn't seem to matter if two or twenty people suddenly wanted something to eat. The dining-room had a placard with the picture of a trout and the words 'Forellen essen nicht vergessen' (don't forget to eat trout). In warm weather we ate outside under a carved balcony or on the terrasse beyond under large coloured sunshades, with an uninterrupted view of the snowy peaks of the Wetterstein range. There was a large St Bernard dog that used to sleep in the sun. There was an ice-house at the back into which they shovelled snow in the winter-time and where they kept the barrels of Lowenbrau beer, so we had frequent litres of dark frothy beer, ice cold to drink, with moisture on the outside of the glass from condensation. In June little boys were sent up the hills to collect wild strawberries, which we ate with sugar and much whipped cream. Herr Demmel, the landlord, looked rather stern, but he was quite the reverse when we got to know him and we used to have great jokes together.

The fishing and any fish that were caught belonged to the Hotel, and unless one wanted to eat the fish, they had to be brought back alive in a wooden water-tank which the Hotel supplied. A fish for eating could either be selected from the tank or killed and brought home, but in either case it had to be paid for on the bill for the meal at which it was eaten. We got into terrible trouble one day. The Loisach was very dirty, so we went fishing with a worm where a clear little stream ran into it. We caught a dirty great grayling which had the worm so far down into its inside that it had to be killed. We didn't want to have to eat the brute, so we gave it away to a spectator and the ungrateful wretch immediately went and told Herr Demmel, who was waiting for us on our return in great anger. We eventually got him calmed down by telling him rather untruthfully that they are regarded as vermin in England and that nobody ever dreamt of eating them!

The wooden tank used to weigh a ton when it had enough water in it to keep a few trout alive, and even with plenty of water, trout died unless the water was continually changed. Rich Germans used to employ diminutive bare-footed boys to carry their tanks for them, but we weren't very rich in those days so we carried it ourselves if we wanted to take any fish home, but it was such a sweat that if we were far from the Hotel we usually killed what we wanted to eat and threw the rest back. If we wanted to take fish back to the Hotel we carried a number of nets like shopping-nets. When we caught a fish we put him in a net and left him there until the evening, when we returned with the tank to collect all the fish and nets. I usually borrowed a bicycle for this job, and many's the mile I have bicycled with a vast wooden tank slung on my back, the water slapping out and running down my coat and shorts, the bicycle protestingly squeaking its rusty way along the hot tarred road.

I believe the French are good fishermen, but the Germans certainly aren't. They usually go fishing in pairs and their minds are seldom entirely occupied with fishing. If one is fishing anywhere near a couple it is advisable to sing or whistle as one walks from one pool to the next, or one may come on the fishing-gear lying idly by the river while gigglings and scufflings are coming from a nearby clump of bushes. The more elderly ones were little better, although, having large wives who only occasionally waddled out to watch the sport, they could give the fishing their undivided attention. Most of them were content to dangle a tired-looking worm in unlikely-looking spots, while some used horrid great black slugs with equally little success; but they always brought home any fish, however small, that was unlucky enough to succumb to these methods, and proudly emptied them into the tank, to be devoured later. I always thought it was rather like a Roman Emperor having a triumph and then murdering the men he had saved up for it. We used to take a few larger trout back to keep Herr Demmel happy and show that we could catch bigger and better fish than the Germans, as we had to uphold British prestige somehow.

The Loisach rises in the high snowfields of the Wetterstein. It has the grey-green colour of snow and glacier water coming from limestone mountains. It is very fast-flowing, and the bottom is all gravel which is constantly moving. I have never known a river alter its course so much from year to year and even from day to day. There may be a pool in a place one year, while the next it is a fast run with no lie for a fish anywhere. The water was always icy-cold in the early morning, but if the sun shone on the valley it soon became quite warm and we used to wade all day without waders in a pair of old shorts and shoes, with the rough water buffeting against our bare knees. The Germans always wore great heavy waders or leather boots and were quite astonished when they saw that we didn't mind getting wet. Usually there was too much colour in the water for fly fishing, so we used to spin with baits and minnows. The best bait was a Miller's Thumb, or 'Koppen' as they were called, which we caught in a clean little stream that came from a spring in a meadow and ran through a small fir wood, then into the Oberau bathing-pool before it entered the main river. We used to go there in the mornings and catch our koppen before starting fishing.

One day Peter found a new-born roe deer calf lying in the

grass of the meadow. It lay quite still as he went up to it to pick it up, and when we put it back again it lay down to wait for its mother.

We kept the baits alive in a tin, killing and mounting them on tackle as we wanted them during the day. I found they were much better fresh and that it wasn't worth fishing with them after the slime had worn off. We also used artificial minnows of various kinds. Some of the most successful Peter manufactured from cloth and painted with oil paints. He made one that was definitely on the stout side and we called it 'Hedda' after a Prima Donna at the Munich Opera House, but I don't think she had much luck.

The Loisach held brown trout, rainbow and grayling, but the majority of fish were rainbow. They used to do very well and grow quite big. They were always in perfect condition and used to play very hard in the fast water, almost as well as sea trout.

For some reason the upkeep of the river banks was the concern of the State Railway. They had become rather worried by the way the river constantly changed its course, so they brought hundreds of tons of rocks and put them along the banks and planted willows on top of them. Peter discovered one day that fish lay all the way down these rocks, and they darted out and took a minnow or small plug bait if it was worked up along the rocks. He put stones along the bank to mark the places where he had moved a fish and I found them in the same spots when I went along later. They were mostly fairly small, the biggest I caught was 1½ lbs, so we used to confine our rock fishing to stretches near the Hotel when we wanted to catch fish to put in the tank, so that we shouldn't have very far to carry them. We used to catch the larger fish in places where there was a pool or any slack water. Some of the best places were opposite a backwater, where the stream crossed over to the bank where the backwater entered the river. The fish would take as the minnow was coming out of the fast water or as it was being worked up the slower-running water between the main stream and the backwater.

There was a place like this where the river ran across to the railway embankment and then alongside it; a deep backwater came in from beside the railway. I fished it one evening when the sun had just gone behind the huge rock which overhangs the western side of the valley here. The far side of the valley was still in the sun. The trees and rocks of the mountain slope beyond, towering to its rugged summit, were softened by its mellow light. The air felt cooler in the shade and the water was surprisingly warm by contrast. I fished it down, carefully wading a step further and deeper with each cast. A train came up the line when I was half-way down the run, the electric engine looking squatly powerful as it came towards me and passed with a violent clatter. The people at the open windows and on the observation platforms waved as they passed. I went on fishing when it had gone and the air was still again, until I was well over my knees in the water. The bait was now fishing the very tail of the slacker water, where the deep strong current ran under the willows and along the rocks of the embankment. I made a final cast, and as the minnow swung into the bank a fish took with a terrific bang and went off with a rush downstream. He was thirty yards away before I could reach the shallower water, which I could only do by wading upstream and away from him. I only had 45 yards of line on my reel, but the backwater was too deep to cross and the willows on the bank would have made playing him from there impossible. Crossing the main river to play him from the shingle of the far bank would have been very difficult as there were four feet of very fast water between myself and the other shore, but if he had kept on going downstream I should have had to try it. Luckily he decided to come back up again, and played around the place where he was hooked, sometimes close under the bushes and sometimes out in the strong current. I didn't see him for about ten minutes, as I was using quite light tackle and couldn't pull at him very hard, but he gradually began to tire. Then I saw that he was a large rainbow. I only had a very flimsy collapsible landing-net, which quite often lived up to its name at the critical moment; but by using it with great care it managed to stand up to the strain this time, and I had him, a lovely deep fish of 3½ lbs with the bright rainbow streak on his clean silvery sides. He was the biggest fish I ever caught out of the Loisach, but I believe I lost one or two which were equally big if not bigger.

Whenever there was any slack water in the pool, snags and various oddments which had been flung into the river higher up used to collect there. The most common snags were old springs from chairs and beds. I must have pulled several hundreds from the bottom of the river. They always felt just like a fish as they came clear of the bottom and the current caught them. There was one place where the current had hollowed out a small hole in the gravel, about five feet deep, and one day I hooked a fish just above this. He bolted downstream into the hole, then the strain went dead. I went down to opposite the fish and looked into the water where the taut line disappeared. I could see the fish flash silver as he turned on his side in the current and he seemed to be attached to some white material which waved about in the stream in about four feet of water. I took off all my clothes except my shoes and shorts, and keeping the line tight with the rod in my left hand, I waded out to the edge of the deep hole and tried to reach the snag with my right hand, but the steep gravel slipped away and in I went overhead. I kept hold of the rod and swam with my right hand until the water became shallower, when I waded ashore. The line was still attached to the fish, so I tried just pulling hard at it, but after a while it broke. I thought this was the end, but before I went I took another look into the depths of the pool and saw that the fish was still attached to the material. Andrew had joined me by this time. He was longer in the arm than I, so I held on to his left hand and he ducked into the water above the fish. As he was being swept past he made a grab for the material with his right hand. He missed it the first time, but the second time he caught it between the bottom and the fish and wrenched it free. The fish was dead from being held in the current by one hook of the triangle, which had become entangled in a large pair of ladies' bloomers; possibly the only time that such an article of clothing had been instrumental in landing a 2 lb rainbow trout.

The river seldom became fit for fly-fishing, for just as it was clearing nicely a tremendous thunderstorm would come rolling down the valley and the river would be a raging torrent and a terrible colour for the next few days. Then there would be another thunderstorm, but occasionally practically all the smoky colour would go and leave the water a clear green. When it was like this it was quite easy to wade across in many places, and by keeping to the inside of the bends one could fish the slack water in the pools all the way down. The larger fish only took a fly in very clear water, and usually they took best in the evening when the sun was off the water. I hooked quite a number but the largest always seemed to get off, as ever. They took a fairly large fly with tinsel on the body best. I generally used a Wickham's Fancy or some such fly, tied as a wet-fly and fished downstream. The current was so fast that fishing upstream for any length of time was quite impossible as one had to cast so often. I remember one good evening at the bottom of the water where the river ran away from the railway, out again into the middle of the flat valley. I caught four rainbows, all over one pound, with the biggest 2 lbs, and hooked and lost several others. I hadn't enough nets for the last one, a fish of 1½ lbs, and I was just going to put it back when a German angler appeared. He was horrified at the suggestion and insisted in carrying it home in his tank. The fine evenings when it forgot to thunder were lovely and cool after the heat of the day. The last rays of the sun fell on the snowfields and pink dolomite peaks of the Zugspitze, as one walked home to a late supper of veal cutlets, fried potatoes and salad followed by the usual strawberries and cream.

Luckily there was another stream to fish when the weather misbehaved and the Loisach was unfishable. The Lauderbach rose on the opposite side of the valley, about a mile from the Hotel. It came from a spring at the foot of the mountains, and was joined by other springs along its whole length. After the first 400 yards it was quite a large stream, and by the time it joined the Loisach two miles down the valley it was as large as the Avon at Amesbury, but much narrower and deeper on the whole. The water was always absolutely clear and very swift-flowing the whole way. The trouble was that it had no banks for most of its length, and ran through a soft bog, which became deeper as one approached the rushes which bordered the river. It only had firm banks for the first half-mile and the last few hundred yards. It was also full of branches, trees, and old bridges which had been washed away and nobody had thought of removing, besides large weed beds, all of which made extracting fish from it no easy matter.

There was a cart track leading to near the source and another that ran down the centre of the valley between the two rivers, but petered out after about a mile. From here the way led through marshy fields and clumps of scrub and pine. In early summer the meadows were blue with the acaulis gentian, and later there were many different kinds of orchis and the air was sweet with the scent of the white butterfly orchis. There was also a later gentian that flowered in July and had several rather paler blue blooms on each stem. The valley was very wild down near the junction of the two rivers and we often saw red deer and roe when we were walking down or standing quietly fishing. There was a hay-barn beside the track to the source of the stream and under it there was a badger's earth. Peter and I were walking back along it one day; he had been sketching and had an umbrella to keep the paints from drying too quickly in the sun. We came around the corner of the hut, to find a young badger going about his natural offices about five yards from the mouth of the hole. Peter was as quick as a knife and got between the badger and the hole and kept him from it with his umbrella until I could catch him in the landing-net. We took him back to the hotel for the night to show to the people there and returned him to the bosom of his family next day. They were very pleased to see him, judging by the squeaks and chattering that went on when he trotted down to join them.

The river held rainbow, brown trout, grayling, chub and river char, but mostly brown trout, and many were of two pounds and over, but once they were hooked they invariably broke the tackle in a weed bed or round a snag. I never managed to land a fish of over 1½ lbs, but one day Maurice appeared with an enormous trout of 2½ lbs which he had outwitted. Apparently it dived into a weed bed immediately it was hooked as usual, and he couldn't get it out again, so he took his clothes off and went in after it with a landing-net. He carefully followed the cast into the weed bed and eventually met up with the fish, which he extracted with the landing-net. The fish took the usual English dry-flies on a slightly larger hook and there was quite a good mayfly rise at the beginning of July for two or three hours every day, which lasted for several weeks. One could usually catch half a dozen trout from ¾ to 1½ lbs in a day, but I always wasted a lot of time trying for the bigger ones and being duly broken when I hooked one. There was one fish in particular of over 2 lbs, fairly near the top of the water. He broke me once using a 4X point and he was shy of 3X gut which made things difficult. He always lay in the same place and waited for the mayfly rise which came on about mid-day: but after he had taken the first few that came over him he became very particular and wouldn't look at an artificial mayfly however skilfully presented. I waited one day for the beginning of the rise. A few mayfly appeared and two or three came floating down until they were in sight of him and then flew away. I suspected that he would be getting pretty angry about this, so I put my fly just above him and he immediately rushed at it with a snap as I had hoped he would. I had him on just long enough to feel him before he was into the rushes on the far side of the stream. There was nobody about, so I rolled my shirt and pullover up under my armpits, took off my shorts, shoes and stockings and armed with a landing-net I went into the icy water. It came above my waist as my feet sank into the soft bottom and it took my breath away; but I waded across and gently felt up the cast among the rushes until I pricked my finger on the fly which was firmly attached to a rush.

There were some large deep pools near the bottom of the river which had schools of chub in them; some were very large and many were over 2 lbs. We noticed one day when there were no trout rising, that after we had peered into the pools for some time the chub seemed to disappear; also when we were wading in the rushes to get near a pool a fish quite often bumped against our legs, so Peter devised what must be a novel way of catching chubs. I stood on one bank and threw things into the pool, while Peter waded quietly into the rushes on the opposite side of the pool and felt around with his hands until he found a fish, which he seized in a firm grip and removed from the river. He caught quite a number, until the chub realised that it was as unhealthy for them in the rushes as out in the pool. I also discovered that chub are sometimes carnivorous. One day I was spinning in the Loisach and reached the bottom of the water, where the Lauderbach joined it, at lunch time. I went over to see if any fish were rising in the Lauderbach, and to prevent my bait from drying in the hot sun I lowered it into the bottom pool which had a number of chub in it. When I picked up the rod after lunch and reeled in the line, I found I had hooked a chub. I tried this from a point of interest in quite a number of other pools and I always hooked a chub. This was borne out by Philip, who once saw an enormous chub biting lumps off a very dead chicken in the river Eamont in Westmorland.

The Lauderbach could have been made a very fine dry-fly stream with a little trouble, if some of the snags had been pulled out and the banks made rather firmer in places, but considering it was never touched it was quite good and we had a lot of fun fishing it.

CHAPTER IX

EARLY DAYS

MY first memory of all is of cold water, for at the age of three I fell into a tub of dirty stagnant rainwater. All I can remember is the breathlessness of going into it head first, and how light it seemed when I sat up in it with my head out of the water and began to yell. Apparently my father was walking in the garden with my mother and had just remarked, as he saw me lean further over to reach for a little boat, 'That child is going to fall in at any moment.' After it happened our Nanny rushed out and put me straight into a hot bath, clothes and all, as the water had been so dirty and I came out black from head to foot. This luckily didn't have the effect of completely frightening me of cold water, although I may not be so keen as some to run over to the washhouse to take a cold shower before breakfast, with only a towel around me when there is snow on the ground and 15 degrees of frost. In fact I never have liked cold showers at all.

I started fishing at Strathaird in the Isle of Skye where we first went when I was four years old, and my brother Maurice seven. It is a perfect place for children, and my father gave us both little greenheart rods; my brother's was bigger than mine as he was rather older. We started fishing on the Kilmarie river which runs close past the house. The sound of its water could be heard from the nursery, and at a very early age we learnt to tell by the noise whether it was in spate or not. The river is usually quite small with a few deep pools, but after a spate it is quite wide and deep and the pools are just smoother patches in the broken water. There is one pool just below the house where a footbridge crosses the river. It is overhung by trees and hazel bushes. Foxgloves and wild raspberries grow on the banks. The water is golden brown when the sun shines on it, from the stain of peat, and although the pool isn't very deep the bottom can't be seen if there is much water coming down. In a big water the river roars over the rocks and under the bridge, which is about 12 feet above the river, and rushes down the far side of the pool and back in a big swirl of brown foam-flecked water under the near bank. It was here that I caught my first fish. We were taken fishing by our Nanny and the keeper, who enjoyed each other's company as much as we enjoyed fishing. Nanny used to put the worms on the hook for us, and we threw them as far as we could out into the fast water and let them come round into the backwater, keeping the line fairly tight so we could feel the first nibble of a fish. When we hooked a fish of any size Nanny used to play it, and she played and landed this first fish of mine which was a brown trout of 1lb. The pool was immediately called Stephen's pool and has been known by that name for the last twenty-six years. I used to be very proud of it.

When we were a little older my brother and I were allowed to go fishing together, while my younger brother Mark went with the keeper, and there was always great rivalry between us. Whenever there was much rain, if there was a puddle on the ground in front of the house there was a good chance of a spate and we used to go to the window on one of the landings at the back of the house to see if the burns were coming down the hill white.

The Kilmarie river is about a mile long from the artificial loch to the sea and it only takes about an hour after heavy rain for the river to rise. It always has a peaty stain, but it never comes down muddy however heavy the rain. If there was a spate we dressed ourselves up in gumboots, mackintoshes and souwesters, and went to the cook for an empty tin to put the worms in. We took it to the gardener and asked him to dig some worms for us. He was often too busy and we had to dig them for ourselves and so we came to know the best places in the little walled kitchen garden in which to look for them. We usually had to find our father and pester him to make us some tackle, but he always loved making things for us children and used to produce the most beautiful single- and double-hooked tackles with slotted leads or shot to weight the line. When everything was ready we set out. Maurice used to carry the rod

The Cuillins (Skye)

as he was the senior partner and I carried the landing-net with the tin of worms in it. We also carried an enormous knife to cut the heads off any eels which we might catch. I wasn't very keen about putting the worms on the hooks and Maurice generally had to do that bit of it, while I held the tin for him and he selected the worm from the wet muddy mass in the bottom of it. Most of the fish we caught were small brown trout, and we kept all but the very smallest, but we quite often caught half-pound sea trout, which we regarded as a great achievement.

We hated catching eels as they made such a slimy mess of the tackle, and we used to think when we hooked the bottom and lost a tackle that it was often an eel that had managed to get under a stone.

We used to start at Stephen's pool and work our way up-stream; the next pool above is the Cornerpool, which fished very well with a worm. The river turns a right-angle and there is a deep hole inside the bend where the worm ends up it, if it is thrown out into the fast water at the head of the pool. A fish often took as the worm was coming out of the faster water. One day Maurice was fishing here and he thought he had hooked the bottom, but he kept on pulling and a great shape floated up from the brown depth of the pool at our feet. It came off at once and sank back again. We thought it was a large brown trout, but now I am sure it must have been a salmon and perhaps it was as well we didn't hook it properly on our little greenheart rod and reel with about 20 yards of line on it.

The bridge pool, where the road to Elgol crosses the river, is just above the corner pool. It fishes very well in a spate with a fly, and my mother once caught nine fish of over a pound out of it in one day, so we weren't much encouraged to fish it with a worm until it had been tried with a fly. A little stream runs into the river at the bottom of the pool, and in a very big water the fish dropped back to below this. A worm dropped into the brawling little burn and allowed to sweep out into the river, was often effective, The worm would go rolling along over the stones and suddenly it would stop and there would be a faint feeling of life at the other end. Very often we raised the rod point to find that the worm had gone and the unsavoury tin had to be consulted again, but sometimes we would be fast in a fat sea trout which went racing out into the stream, making the little reel screech its high note and the rod bend double. We caught quite a number of fish from this one spot when we discovered it, but the main pool was best in a rather lower water. One day Maurice hooked a large fish in it and played it for some time. It must have weighed about 2 lbs, but it eventually got off. I insisted on calling the pool Maurice's pool for a long time after that, as it seemed unfair that I should have a pool named after me and he shouldn't just because he had lost his fish!

Above the bridge pool is the Church pool, which is the deepest pool in the river. We weren't allowed to go near it unless we had the keeper with us, as my mother was afraid that we might fall in and be drowned, and we were very good about not going there. There was only one other pool between here and the loch. It was out on the moor and called the Bend pool; but we seldom reached it before it was time to go home and get a meal. There were big stones and ledges of rock in it where we lost quite a number of tackles.

It is strange how one still loves doing things that one did as a child, and when I'm at Strathaird I practically always have a try with a worm if there is a big spate. We were only there for four days last summer, but I managed to try the bridge pool with a worm on one of them. I wouldn't dream of fishing for sea trout with a worm anywhere else, chiefly because one doesn't usually catch so many fish that way.

The first fish I ever caught by casting a fly was on the Leven in Yorkshire. I used to go down and watch my father fishing as often as possible. One day he asked me if I would like to try, and gave me the rod. I think I was about six at the time. I had watched him fishing so often that I found it fairly easy and threw quite a reasonable line with instructions from him. I caught a fish in the first run I tried. It must have been quite tiny as even to me it looked small, and when my father suggested that it was hardly big enough to keep I reluctantly agreed and put it back.

I can still see him standing by the river and asking with a smile whether I wanted to keep it. He was as pleased as I was that I had managed to catch a fish casting.

Soon after that he gave me the little split-cane rod that he used for fishing the Leven and I used it until a few years ago. I had sat on it and trodden on it; it had two splices and a new top joint and a decided kink to starboard at one of the splices which made ominous noises when one cast; but I must have caught many hundred brown trout and over a thousand sea trout on it during the time I used it.

Fly-fishing opened up tremendous new vistas, as far as Strathaird was concerned, as even before I could go over the hill to Camasunary and fish on a loch for the whole day I had watched my mother and father fishing the river and loch at Kilmarie many a time and I knew how to go about it. My mother used to fish Stephen's pool upstream when a spate ran in. We used to stalk down together, keeping to the far side of the bridge from the pool. We crouched down and walked as quietly as possible when we crossed it, to avoid disturbing the fish. She went round below and came up under the bank, while I climbed up into a hazel bush high above the river to watch. Presently I would hear the reel as she let the line out, and then the line and fly would fall lightly across the pool and the fly move downstream in little jerks. It was a great point of vantage and I could always see the fish come wriggling up from the brown depth and turn at the fly with a flash of silver. I used to whistle when I saw one rise, and if she hadn't seen it she struck when she heard me whistle. I used to get very excited and implore her to put the fly on to the place in the pool where I thought most of the fish were lying. When she hooked a fish I could see every kick and turn it made until it went out of sight downstream and was netted. She quite often used to catch half a dozen fish in succession. I expect I was continually pestering her to go out fishing when she had other important things to do.

We usually went to Strathaird in July and from then on I spent as little time as possible doing lessons and as much as possible fishing. The result was that I could fish much better than I could read or write when I was nine years old and it was time for me to go to school; but unfortunately the masters didn't seem to realise that being able to fish was an asset. My mother was rather worried about this and went to the trouble of taking me to an occulist to see if my eyes were the reason that I couldn't learn to read, but he pronounced my eyes as perfect and suggested that perhaps I was just lazy, which was nothing but the case.

After I had my fly-rod I used to fish the artificial loch at Kilmarie practically every morning unless the keeper was wanted for something else. It is quite a small loch with a dam at one end and is about thirty feet deep at the centre. It is shallow round the edges with weed banks close to the shore, and two fairly large burns run into it. It holds hundreds of small brown trout and sea-trout fry, and quite a number of sea trout mostly small but running up to 8 lbs, with an occasional small salmon or grilse. Most of the fish I caught were brown trout, but I quite often caught a half-pound sea trout. Maurice and I had often rowed the boat for our mother so we knew the best places to fish. Whenever I caught a sea trout I used to be very proud as I took it home to show to the family.

I remember one day on the pond after there had been a good spate. The burns were still coming white down Slatbhein and the sound of running water was loud as we walked up to the loch. The burn running in from Corrie Ballach and the Happy Valley was still big and foam-flecked water reached well out into the loch. This used to be a very good place in a high water, and Macky as we called Peter MacIntyre, the keeper, worked the boat up to one side of the channel through the weed while I fished across it. I didn't touch a fish as we went up, and I was idly casting a fly across it as we went down again, when a fish took the fly. He kept deep, and luckily followed the boat down through the narrow channel in the weeds until we reached the open water beyond. Once we were clear of the weeds he made a terrific rush and jumped about 40 yards away. He looked enormous to me, and he must have been over 4 lbs, a very big fish for a little boy of seven to play, but he soon got off. I remember

I burst into tears! I have often felt like doing so since, but I have had to express my feelings by the less satisfactory method of swearing.

Most of the fishing at Strathaird is three miles from Kilmarie house where we lived, over a hill 600 ft high, at Camasunary. There is another little house at Camasunary and the river runs quite close to it. A mile up the valley towards Sligachan is Loch na Creitach, which is just over a mile long, and another mile beyond is the smaller Loch an Athain. The first time I went over the hill to Camasunary I rode behind my brother on a pony called Flora. We were very small and there was plenty of room for us both on the same felt pad while our Nanny walked. I can remember being rather cross that I had to sit behind and that I wasn't allowed to steer, but Maurice didn't do much steering either, as Flora was an old stag pony and had been over the same path hundreds of times. The path leaves the road to Elgol about half a mile from the bridge and branches off along the face of Meabost above the loch. After the loch is passed it dips into a hollow and then climbs up over a spur of Slatbhein, about 600 ft high. At first a few peaks of the Cuillins are visible over the spur, but after the path goes into the hollow they are hidden until the top of the hill is reached, when the whole range comes into view. The far side of the hill leading down to Camasunary is much steeper then the Kilmarie side, and from the top of the hill the bay seems to be at one's feet. There is a wide crescent of sand between the sparkling sea and the green grass of the park. The house looks tiny from the top of the hill, with the pony path winding down among rocks and heather and leading up to it. Beyond the valley rises the dark mass of Sgur na Strie and Corrie dubh, the dark corrie, while above and beyond them are the clear blue peaks of the Cuillins. Out to sea are the islands of Soay and Canna, with Rhum in the distance, and on a very clear day the outer isles can be seen. On a calm day it is always very quiet when one pauses on the top of the hill, with only the faint sound of trickling water and the distant noise of the sea as the swell lazily breaks and spreads across the sand. It is my favourite view. I have seen it hundreds of times and my only regret is that I shall never be able to see it for the first time. The last time I stood on the top of the hill was on a Sunday morning in the Summer of 1942, when I had been recalled from leave by telegram. I never saw it look as lovely with the whole scene bathed in sunlight.

During the summer holidays we used to have many people to stay, but we usually had the first fortnight by ourselves and the whole family went over the hill to stay at Camasunary. The only way of reaching it is by the pony path or by going about 12 miles round by sea, and it meant a good deal of arranging for the whole family to move. Sheets, coal, clothes, food and a cow, all had to get there somehow. The heavy items like coal went round by sea, while the cow walked, and the daily supplies either came in panniers on a pony or in a game bag on the keeper's back. This isn't such a good way for carrying a raspberry tart, as we once discovered. It was a perfect place for boys as there were hundreds of rabbits in the park and fishing in the sea or in the river and lochs. Loch Coruisk is only two miles away by sea. We often used to go there on fine days trailing for lythe with handlines on the way there and back.

The day we rode on Flora we fished the fisherman's pool with worms. My brother caught one or two but I don't believe I caught anything. We soon began fishing with flies. Maurice used to prefer shooting rabbits with a ·410, but I would always rather fish than shoot, and I used to go on fishing until my little arms ached.

The Camasunary river has only one pool in it which always holds sea trout, the fisherman's pool, which the sea just reached on a very high spring tide. Below this is a broad stretch which we called 'the flat', which sometimes fishes very well in a high water when fish are running. I remember my father fishing the flat one day in a good spate. It needed a long cast to hook a fish. Maurice and I couldn't quite reach them, but my father let us play the ones he hooked. He hooked and we played about ten half-pound sea trout and then he hooked a much bigger one which he played himself. We were very excited as we watched him playing the fish, and Maurice landed it for him, a sea trout of about $3\frac{1}{2}$ lbs. They all had sea lice on them and were swimming straight out of the sea.

Below the flat is the sea pool, which has short seaweed on the stones. The tide enters it at about three-quarter full water. It usually holds fish unless the water is dead low, and it was an easier place for a small boy to fish as the fish lie fairly close in to the nearer shore when the tide is out of the pool. A fly thrown out into the fast water works round very nicely and a sea trout often takes just as it is coming into the slack water at the edge. After I had fished it down once or twice I used to cast the fly as far out into the stream as I could and then run upstream along the bank holding the rod as far out over the river as possible. I found this was very effective and I caught quite a number of fish in this way.

It was here that I first learnt how easy it is to knock the barb off a hook on the stones behind as one is casting. I lost many a fish before I learnt to look at the fly whenever I missed or lost a fish. When I could only throw a fairly short line the fish seemed more than ever to lie under the far bank and be just beyond my reach. The first good catch I had was in the sea pool one day when the rest of the family were fishing on the lochs. I was only eight at the time and I had a ghillie with me to see I didn't drown myself. I caught eight half-pound sea trout in the sea pool, some by fishing normally and some by running up the bank. I had only fished the near side of the pool, but whenever I managed to throw an extra long line it seemed that I rose a fish, so I decided that they were all over the far side of the run and that if only I could get there I should be able to catch them. There were some very bad stepping-stones just above the pool and few remained from the winter spates, but I wanted to get to the other side very badly, so I suggested to the ghillie that he should carry me across. He seemed a bit dubious, but eventually he set out carrying the rod and net with myself on his back clutching him round the neck. All went well for the first few stones, but then they became very far apart and slippery, and one tilted up just as he put his weight on it. He tried to save himself but down we went. Luckily the water wasn't very deep and we didn't get very wet, but he was terribly concerned about it as he wrung the water out of my clothes! I started fishing from the far bank full of hope and I was astonished to find that I didn't rise a single fish. When the tide is in the pool it can fish quite well from this bank, but otherwise it is no use at all. We crossed back safely and I was a very proud little boy as I walked back to the house with my eight sea trout, the water squelching in my shoes.

The fisherman's pool is a really wonderful sea-trout pool, but it has to be fished upstream and across with a fairly long line. When I started I wasn't able to manage it. It always holds sea trout from the beginning of July until mid-October, but it fishes best in August and early September. It isn't at all unusual to catch over twenty fish from it in a day. The water is absolutely clear as it runs from the igneous rocks of the Cuillins and Blaven. My mother always caught more fish than most people, as she crouched down when she approached and sat on the bank to fish. I used to sit on a knoll above the pool and watch her fishing. Fish were continually jumping and one could often see the flash of silver as a fish turned deep below the surface. When she hooked one I used to run down and stalk up beside her to net it for her. She usually kept me quite busy.

We were too young to go night fishing in those days and the day ended with supper in our pyjamas and dressing-gowns, glasses of milk and biscuits. There was always an enormous box of assorted biscuits with all kinds of exciting varieties, and we used to sit round the peat fire eating them and listening to the sound of the wind and sea, and the splatter of rain on the window before we went off to our beds.

CHAPTER X

SEA TROUT IN THE SEA

A FEW of the larger sea trout begin coming into the sea lochs round Skye towards the end of May and early in June, but the majority appear during July. These are the big fish weighing from 3 to 14 lbs, which have already returned to the river, where they were bred, several years in succession, since sea trout return to fresh water every year after their first migration to the sea.

The larger ones have probably spawned once or twice in the little streams at the head of the river system up which they run. They are wise in the way of the sea and know its many dangers. A big fish often carries scars, narrow escapes from the teeth of seals and conger eels. He knows the feel of a net, and avoids bag nets in which a salmon will be caught, for he has learnt much cunning in his yearly journeys to the sea to feed, and back to the rivers and lochs to mate and breed in the Autumn. Once the big fish come into the estuary they waste no time in running up the rivers if there is enough water, and in a normal year only an occasional big fish is seen in the bays after the end of July. The smaller fish, or Finnochs, weighing from ½ to 1 lb, begin to appear in the middle of July, but the majority run in August and September. The first big run is often around August 12th, and I have frequently spent a much more profitable day fishing than the rest of the party who chased the very odd and usually half-grown grouse.

As a rule the big fish don't show much in the bays and there is little opportunity to observe them in the sea, but in 1933 there was no spate from mid-June until August. I arrived at Strathaird early in July, to find the rivers mere trickles and the bays at Camasunary and Scavaig full of fish anxious to run up to Loch na Creitach and Coruisk. From the top of the hill above Camasunary one could see the splashes of jumping fish at the mouth of the river, half a mile away and 600 feet below. I told A. this, but he didn't believe a word of it until we stood for a moment on the top of the hill. It was half-tide, with a crescent of wet sand stretched from the green grass to the sea which sparkled in the sunlight. We saw splash after splash on the calm surface although we were too far off to see the fish. A. was so excited that he started running down the hill. It was an admirable opportunity to watch their behaviour in salt water, but most exasperating trying to catch fish in the dead-calm sea with only a slight swell drifting the fronds of seaweed to and fro, and a brilliant sun casting heavy shadows day after day.

The water in the Camasunary estuary is very shallow. At low tide shingle and sand stretch several hundred yards out to sea. There were fish jumping somewhere at practically all times of day and night.

When sea trout are out at sea on their feeding-grounds they may well go alone and keep far apart from one another, but when they congregate in a bay they move about in shoals. The larger fish keep together and usually away from the smaller ones although there is considerable overlapping. When the tide came into the sea pool and spread out over the broad stretch of flat shingle above it, the fish would follow it hopefully feeling their way into the fresh water. As the tide dropped back they reluctantly went with it. The very large fish would keep further out than the smaller ones, and if they did enter the sea pool in daytime they left in plenty of time to avoid being stranded. They come up more confidently at night than in the bright daylight, and the fresher fish, straight from the deep sea, were keener to try to run up the river than the staler fish which had been hanging about the estuary for several weeks. Towards the end of July the staler fish became rather red and could be seen jumping away out in the bay, never bothering to come into the river mouth at all.

As the tide fell away the river water flowed over a bar of shingle which had patches of seaweed about 2 ft. long growing on the stones, so that there was a stretch of seaweed on the sur-

Mouth of Coruisk River (Skye)

face between the shore and the deeper water beyond. We quite often saw a great tail or dorsal fin lazily waving about among the weed, as the swell washed gently backwards and forwards. When the tide was dead low the fish moved out into deeper water and could be seen jumping well out to sea, but they used not to show so much for an hour either side of low water. Most fish seemed to show at half-tide, when they were moving into or out from the river mouth and were in fairly shallow water. Quite often several would jump within the space of a minute straight up into the air and back with a splash which broke the silence and sent spray flying.

In Scavaig the sea runs in beneath the Cuillins, and Garsbheinn rises three thousand feet sheer from the waters of the bay, its jagged outline of black rock bold against the sky. Loch Coruisk is hidden from the sea by a shoulder of rock, although the river is only three hundred yards long, and the drop from the loch to the sea at high tide not more than twenty feet. Deep water runs right up to the river, which empties its crystal-clear water over a glacially smooth slab of black rock straight into the sea. At high tide the sea is level with the top of the rock, and only at low tide a few seaweed-covered boulders at the base of the rock are uncovered, which shelve steeply into deep sea. Stretching out on either side of the river are other rocks dipping into deep water and forming a small bay. The rainfall in Coruisk is the highest for any place in the British Isles, but this year there wasn't even enough water for the fish to swim the short distance to the loch, although they tried, as Lachy the ghillie found a small shoal of huge fish half-way up and practically out of water; but they had to turn back again.

There were thousands of sea trout in Scavaig but in the deep water off the mouth of the river they didn't show quite as much as at Camasunary. They kept in shoals, sometimes keeping deep down over the green sand and purple seaweed for a long time, and then coming near the surface where they would break the water or jump. There was one shoal or there might have been more than one, but we often saw one in much the same place which always consisted of giant fish. They would dimple the surface like dace and then several would jump, falling back with resounding splashes. They were all over eight pounds and many very much larger, as far as we could judge. We spent many profitless hours trying to catch them.

Our problem was to catch these fish. We tried fishing the lochs but there weren't enough fish up to make it worth while, and we soon realised that the complete stocks of both river systems were in the sea off the mouths of the rivers. We tried fishing from a boat, but the sea was so clear and the light so bright that we could seldom get within casting distance of a fish, especially at Camasunary, where the boat threw a distinct shadow on the bottom of the shallow water; although the first day I arrived I caught a fish with my first cast from the boat and immediately thought I was going to have the time of my life.

We fished most of the time at Camasunary as we were staying there. At high tide we could fish the narrow neck below the sea-pool from the steep shingle banks; further up in the pool we could also cover most of the water from the shore. A. was fishing the neck one day as the tide began to ebb, when he saw a sea trout of about 4 lbs swim serenely past at his feet. He frantically shortened his line and put his fly just in front of it, but it paid not the slightest attention and went swimming out to sea.

When the tide left the pool we used to wade out along the shingle bar until we were standing in a clearing at the edge of the seaweed, and cast out into the ebbing water beyond. As the tide fell we waded further out, to keep just beyond the fringe of the seaweed that reached to the surface of the water. The sun was so hot and the water so warm that we waded for hours in our shirtsleeves and without waders. I usually wore an old pair of shorts and gym-shoes, and if I wanted to go in very deep I took off my shorts and rolled my shirt and pullover up under my armpits, making sure there were no female hikers about until I was deep enough to be decent. The salt water made one's legs tingle, as it flowed past, clear for a moment and then cloudy where fresh water mingled with the salt and twisted the light, making the stones at one's feet momentarily indistinct.

The fish came down on the tide and out over the bar in shoals. For a time there would be no fish within reach; although there were always some jumping further out in the bay, nothing would follow the fly. Then a fish would jump close to the seaweed, just above where one was standing, and within a minute the shoal would be within reach of a long cast. Very often if a fly fell within sight of a fish a smooth bow wave would appear on the glassy surface just behind the fly as one pulled the line in through the rings. We found it best to throw a long line out and work the fly in little jerks right up to our feet by pulling in the line through the rings. We used a greased line to give us more control over a long line. If a wave followed a fly it was no good working it more slowly to give the fish a chance to catch it up as the fish immediately lost interest; but if the fly was speeded up the fish sometimes made a grab at it. The fish generally turned away without taking, but sometimes one would snatch at the fly as it turned and then the fun began. The line, which had been pulled in through the rings and lay in coils on the surface of the water and among the seaweed at one's feet, had to be played out until it ran directly from the reel to the first ring; while a very fresh and indignant sea trout made mad rushes in every direction and sent spray flying as it thrashed the surface or flung itself into the air in a frantic struggle to escape the restraining pull on its mouth.

Luckily a hooked fish made no attempt to escape in the seaweed even if there was a forest just beneath the surface, and if they were well hooked we usually landed them; but we hooked very few. It was all the more tantalising, as we kept seeing enormous fish jumping or showing within easy reach, and a fly dropped near a big fish often produced a large bow wave which followed the fly for several yards. I firmly believed that the wave approaching the fly was made by a single fish, until one day, when I was fishing from a fairly high rock in Scavaig. Some fish showed within reach, and next cast a wave came towards the fly and followed right in below the rock. The light was just right so that I could see the fly in the water. Then I saw the 'fish'. About two feet behind the fly, making no attempt to overtake it, were about a dozen fish varying from about four to eight pounds in weight.

We found that very small bright flies were the best for these fish, but weather conditions made catching them exceptionally difficult. A sudden gust of wind or shower of rain made a big difference, but there were all too few of them. The sun went in for a moment and the wind rose and blew a squall of rain from the Cuillins one day when I was fishing Scavaig from a boat anchored opposite the mouth of the river. Unfortunately the shoal of really big fish didn't appear within reach, but there were some smaller ones about. I caught five averaging two pounds before the wind dropped and the sun shone again on a calm blue sea. In normal years when there is plenty of wind and rain sea trout are easier to catch in the sea. They take an artificial sand-eel, made of soleskin painted blue and silver, very well.

We fished at all times of day and night; but we did best in the sea pool and narrow neck just below, in the evening when the tide was high, or beginning to ebb.

We lived a perfect life at Camasunary house, sleeping when we were tired and eating when we were hungry. We usually got up fairly late and had a large breakfast of porridge and fried sea trout. We spent the day fishing or stalking rabbits in the park with a rifle, with a snack for lunch. In the evening we had another meal of sea trout and raspberry tart or anything else that had been sent over the hill from Kilmarie.

We went out fishing again when the sun was low and the shadow of the mountains stretched darkly across half the valley. The river would be already in shadow, and as we walked across the green park we would go suddenly from warmth of sunshine to the cool of shade, as the last rays of the sun sparkled momentarily on the black mountain peak. The grass was always alive with rabbits and we often saw hinds and calves which had come down to feed on the good grass. They would raise their heads and look at us as we passed within a few hundred yards, until an old hind gave her dry warning cough, when they would turn and gallop off with their high stiff action. They never went very far before they stopped and stared at us and they would be feeding again when we were still in sight. Further up the valley the sun still shone on Blaven and Marsco, turning the granite a deep red against the pale sky, while out to sea the Island of Rhum was a pale blue in a calm sea.

We usually fished one on either side of the river, fishing the sea pool or the neck below it and following the shoals of fish as they showed up and down the river. We had a boat handy at the mouth in case something very large was hooked and had a mind to make for the open sea again.

It was very quiet in the evenings. There were no streams chattering and gurgling down the mountain, as they had long dried up to tiny trickles that only whispered their way down to the sea. The calm sea lapped the stones with scarcely a sound. Only the splash of a fish jumping or a quiet voice from the opposite bank broke the stillness of the night. As it grew dark, outlines on the opposite bank became indistinct and merged into the dark background of the mountains. The darkest part of the night was from 12.30 to 1.30, but it never became too dark to see reflections of light, from ripples on the inky black surface, made by rings of rising fish. These spread across the river, although one often saw a rise too late to strike. The fish took quite differently at night. There was never a sudden snatch at the fly; but as it was being worked towards the bank a slight draw would be felt as though a piece of weed had touched it. If one struck quickly enough there would be a heavy weight for a second before the fish made off, tearing the line from the reel and flinging itself into the air, breaking the still of the night with the noise of the reel and splashing of water, and sending ripples of light in all directions over the surface. Too often they came off in the first mad rush as fresh sea trout seem to have very tender mouths; but we landed quite a number. The smaller fish, up to about three pounds, were landed from the bank without difficulty; but if a large one was hooked the sound of the reel would continue and there would be frantic cries for the boat, followed by the scraping of wood on shingle and the rhythmic thump of oars in rowlocks as the boat put out to sea.

As the tide ebbed and the water became shallower the sport

became brisker, since the smaller fish were reluctant to leave until the seaweed had appeared and the tide had left the pool. We usually caught half a dozen or more fish an evening, averaging 2 lbs; but we never managed to land anything bigger than 6 lbs, although some of the fish that went rushing off into the darkness with the reel screaming may have been any size.

One Saturday the tide was just right, so A. and I carefully left our watches behind before setting out in the evening and hoped that Lachy the ghillie had done the same. We had a good evening's fishing and A. hooked a big fish during the darkest part of the night. After the sound of much running and scrambling on the other bank he put to sea after it and the noise of the oars grew faint until it disappeared into the black distance. I went on fishing for some time and caught two more fish before it began to get light. Then I sat on the bank and lit a pipe to wait for A., thinking he would be back any moment however large a fish he had hooked. I had to wait a further half an hour before he returned in broad daylight with a 6½lb sea trout. When they had landed I tactfully looked up at the sky and said: 'My goodness, it must be nearly Sunday.' Lachy replied: 'Och, and I thought it would be Monday before we would be back.'

As a rule the fish have no difficulty in getting into the lochs as the Cuillins are the first mountain barrier to the wet Atlantic winds, and force them up into the colder air, causing precipitation so that the rainfall is exceptionally high. This was the only opportunity I have had for observing a big concentration of large fish in the bays; but later in the season, in August and September, when the smaller fish are running, a few days without a spate are sufficient to concentrate a large number round the mouths of the rivers. The smaller fish aren't quite so keen to reach the lochs, and even when there are a series of good spates, a number will hang around the sea pool and river mouth at Camasunary. They behave in much the same way as the bigger fish, but they seem keener to come into the sea pool and broad water above, especially on a big spring tide. They show quite a lot as the tide is flowing, but at high tide there may be no sign of a fish for half an hour or so.

On a high tide small parties of fish sometimes work their way up the hundred yards of very shallow water into the fisherman's pool, even when the river is dead low and their backs are well clear of the water; but most of the fish remain in the salt water and drop back on the tide. A cousin of mine once found an 8-lb salmon trying to swim up in about 3 inches of water. It was doing quite well, until he saw it; but it didn't get very far after that. It is still the only salmon to be taken in the Camasunary river. I believe he used his hat to take it in.

I remember one day in August fishing the shallow between the broadwater and the seapool as the tide was ebbing. There had been no sign of life when the tide was full, so I didn't think there were many fish about until they started to drop back again. There wasn't more than three feet of water opposite where I was fishing and it was a glassy calm except for the dimples made by sea trout which covered the whole stretch about 40 yards broad by 100 yards long. The tide was running out at about three miles an hour, and for half an hour there were fish showing. Practically every cast I made during this time moved at least one fish, and very often separate waves dashed at the fly from every direction. If one fish turned and missed another would have a go and another, until the fly was practically on the land. The midges were awful and became embedded in my homespun stockings. I was trying to scratch my legs against each other most of the time as I couldn't spare a hand from the fishing. I caught twelve fish in the half-hour before the tide had ebbed leaving the shingle bare. They were mostly small ¾-lb fish, but I caught one of 1½ lbs and one of 2½ lbs, and there were occasional larger fish about.

At the narrow neck below the pool it is often possible to see a shoal of fish in the water if the light is right; especially if they give their whereabouts away by dimpling the surface. It is most entertaining watching about a dozen fish following the fly, as they will often come right up to one's feet before they turn away again. If the fly falls near a shoal, a fish usually makes a grab at it before it has gone very far, but very often it is a quick snatch as the fish turns away, which just bends the rod point before the fish has gone again. We have found that a very small and extremely sharp hook is the best for hooking these fish, and the tiny bright flies used in greased-line fishing for salmon in dead-low water are as good as anything.

It is always great fun catching a number of fish in a short time, especially if one has been fishing a loch for larger fish for many hours with little success. The mouth of the Coruisk river is usually worth a cast or two on the way to and from Loch Coruisk if the tide is about half-full. We stand by the river mouth where the water breaks white over the smooth rock and splashes down into the sea, and fish out into the current which moves sluggishly into the little bay.

On the far side of the river and just level with the sea at high tide there is a small pot-hole in the rock, not more than five yards in diameter and three feet deep, which is sometimes blue with sea trout. It is all too easy to poach with a net and I expect thousands of fish have been taken from it in the past. One can usually catch two or three from it with a fly before the fish begin to resent seeing a flopping sea trout dragged up over the rocks; but if one goes near enough to land one with a net the rest are put down immediately. We frequently catch a dozen or so from the sea when they are running, but Mark was once there when the big fish were running. He could see them jumping the falls, and they simply wouldn't look at his fly.

There is a very large stock of sea trout at Coruisk and Camasunary now as poachers have been discouraged for a number of years, but we still have a bit of fun from time to time. One night in the year 1933 I was sitting by the mouth of the river at Camasunary having a pipe after catching half a dozen fish when a mysterious boat appeared out of the darkness and said they were looking for 'herrin's'. We weren't satisfied, so we rowed out after them and found they had put a net across the mouth of the river a hundred yards out. Although we were outnumbered we eventually persuaded them to remove it by retiring ashore and flinging stones at them. The tide had fallen when we rowed back up the river and for the last 200 yards there was only about 2 ft of water. An oar splashed and the whole surface was broken by fish splashing and racing out to sea past the boat. It was impossible to estimate their number, but there must have been nearly a thousand; anyway I hate to think how many would have caught the morning train from Mallaig to London if we hadn't been there.

CHAPTER XI

SEA TROUT IN RIVERS

'EARLY to river and late to loch' is a saying which I have often heard, and I suspect it of being as fallacious as many things that 'they' say. It is difficult to know who is master of misinformation behind some of the damned silly things that 'they' do say, which a moment's thought would show to be quite impossible. For instance they say that when a ship sinks in very deep water it never reaches the bottom. Also that a swan can break a man's leg with its wing—what nonsense, and yet most people accept this as true. They also used to say when I was a boy, that if one fell from an aeroplane one was dead before one hit the ground. It is very lucky for most people here that this isn't true, however dead one may be a very short time after one hits the ground.

To revert to fishing, I was once mug enough to believe the saying sufficiently to get out of a comfortable bed at four o'clock on an August morning and go out fishing on the Kilmarie river. There was a feeling of unreality about the place as I slipped out of the quiet house into the cold yellow light of early sunshine and walked down to the river with my rod and landing-net. Nothing stirred except the midges, which devoured me alive at the first pool I fished. Smoking was no use for keeping them off and I had to return to the house to find something more effective. All I could find was a tin of 'Flit'. I must have been pretty dim, possibly owing to the time of the day, for I had heard that 'They' had said it was the thing for protection against midges, and I fell for it. I covered my face, neck and hands with the stuff and even took the tin with me to anoint myself from time to time as it wore off. It was certainly most effective, for as soon as midges landed in it, they had had it, and I was soon a dirty grey from a thin covering of dead midges.

It had rained early in the night so there was a good water in the river; the pools were a golden brown in the early light with white foam below the falls, and it seemed a very good chance of catching sea trout. I fished all the pools up to the loch very carefully, but I never caught anything except a few minute brown trout which I put back. I fished the best pools on my way back to the house, with equally little success and it was only 6.30 when I went indoors. My face was beginning to feel rather sore, so I washed it at once. After that there was absolutely nothing to do until breakfast at 8.30. I was too wide awake to go to sleep again, and anyway my face and neck became more and more painful until they were hurting like mad. I was made to realise very forcibly that pure paraffin is not the best thing to rub into tender skin and leave on for a couple of hours. Luckily the skin didn't blister but it was very tender for a couple of days and ever since I have been very suspicious of everything that 'they' say.

The Kilmarie river can be great fun in a spate and fishes best in August or September after the river has been low for some time. It isn't so good if there is much rain and the river is in spate day after day. The river runs down amazingly quickly and begins to fall about an hour after the heavy rain stops, as the loch is too small to keep the river full for any length of time. It is never dirty, however heavy the rain may be, but there is always a faint brown stain of peat in the summer-time which practically disappears in the winter. I have fished every little corner and hole since I was a boy, with worms, minnows and flies; and I always have a morning on the river, where a different height of water means varying tactics in every pool.

The sea pool below the boat-house is worth a cast if the tide is low and the river not too big. It is a fast run with slack water at either side where the fish lie, and it changes its shape every year as the shingle banks are moved by the winter storms. At low tide seaweed-covered stones and shingle stretch down to the sea and beyond are the distant blue hills of Sleat. The smell of salt and the cry of sea birds are in the air. If a fly is cast right across the run a fish usually takes it, either just as it leaves the slack water beyond the stream or as it reaches the slack water on the near side of the pool and hangs for a moment. There is a swirl in the rough brown water and a fierce tug as the fish turns with the fly. Sea trout won't lie in very fast water. At the head of a pool they generally lie in the slack at the edges of the run; but further down a pool where the main stream is easier, and at the tail of a pool they generally lie well out in the middle. Stephen's pool is too big to fish upstream in a spate, but the tail is worth a cast downstream. The fish take where the water runs in a smooth glide under the trees, and the rocks are just visible through the brown water. The run just below also fishes very well in a good water; but it is difficult to fish, as tall bracken and wild raspberries cover the bank from which one fishes, and branches of trees growing on the opposite bank sweep the water with their green leaves. The fly works round very nicely and one can usually see it in the water and watch the fish materialise from the depth below it. It is difficult not to strike too soon, but if one doesn't there is usually a fat sea trout kicking on the other end of the line a second later. The snags on the bank make landing a fish here difficult.

All the pools hold finnocks, as they will rest in any little bit of slack water when they run up the river. Some of these places are too small to fish with a fly, but it is worth dropping a worm into any deep, slack piece of water. We used to catch fish from the most unlikely-looking places, as sea trout differ from salmon in that they will take while they are actually running. We used to work our way downstream with a worm trickling along the bottom, and sometimes caught sea trout in the fastest of water. I remember catching one where the river ran very swiftly in a bend over a smooth rock. There was no break in the water or resting-place for a fish, so that it must have been running all the time.

There are only two deep pools which often hold bigger fish than finnocks, the Bridge pool and the Church pool. The Bridge pool fishes best upstream except in a very big spate. The first good cast is always most exciting. The line is gradually lengthened and the fly falls further and further up the pool until it lands over the deep black water. It is best to work it back downstream in little jerks, moving it rather faster than the flow of the river. The fish usually takes just at the bottom edge of the deep, as the fly is coming on to the shallow; there is a swirl and flash of silver and the little rod bends double. The reel purrs as the fish runs upstream, leaving a widening ring on the smooth-flowing surface. My mother was always very fond of this pool and she used to catch a number of fish of a pound and over from it during the summer. I fished it one day late in the season and I rose and touched a large fish fairly hard, which went off with a big swirl. In the afternoon I fished the pool again and caught a fish of 4 lbs in exactly the same place. I think it was the same fish, as one of this size is unusual in the Bridge pool unless it is running through to the loch early in the season.

Most of the larger fish run straight through to the loch, but a certain number drop back in the Autumn and run up the little burns which enter the river below the loch to spawn. The loch is artificial and was made about forty years ago. There are plenty of good burns running into it, affording ample space for the whole stock of sea trout to spawn, but one still meets these fish dropping back in the Autumn. There is one very favourite little burn entering the river just below the Bridge pool; I believe generation after generation of sea trout have spawned in it and their offspring follow in their parents' paths and go back to the spot where they were hatched to spawn.

On another occasion I hooked a fish of about two pounds in the Bridge pool on a fly, and played him for some time. I saw him several times, a very red fish. He had probably also dropped back from the loch. He eventually left the pool when he was practically played out and was washed downstream in the fast brown water. I followed as best I could but he got off about forty yards below the pool. In the afternoon I went out with a minnow and fished a little pool below the bridge pool. In low water it was no pool, but in a spate there is some slack water where a running finnock often rests. I hooked a very red fish the first cast; he didn't play at all and came straight to the net. I am sure it was the same fish, as this was the first place it could have stopped after leaving the Bridge pool in an exhausted condition. I suppose he wanted a good feed to build up some body energy, or perhaps he wanted to get some of his own back on a defenceless member of his own breed.

The Church pool is the deepest in the river and is the only pool to hold big fish all through the season. It sometimes fishes very well in a big water and my father used to catch a number of fish from it, but I have never done much good there. Just above the pool the river runs through a narrow rocky channel and falls into the pool with a roar of white water. The whole surface of the pool is covered with foaming water and frothy bubbles of spray. The bigger the water the better it fishes. They take right in the foaming water, but the water a few feet below the surface must be much stiller. Landing a fish single-handed is the difficulty as the bank is very high and steep, and it is almost essential to have an accomplice to scramble down the bank with the landing-net.

It only takes a morning to fish the whole river, but one often goes back to lunch with half a dozen sea trout, mostly finnocks of about ½ to ¾ lb, but with an occasional fish of 1 or 2 lbs. It is best when there are plenty of fish in the bay running up the river, and when it rains off and on all day so that the river is kept fairly high. After it stops raining the river runs in very rapidly and is too low within a few hours.

One very wet 12th August I magnanimously said I would stay behind while the rest of the party went off by car to Sligachan to shoot grouse on a very remote and extremely bad piece of moor. They shot three grouse and a grey hen while I caught twenty-three sea trout. I fished with a worm for a short time when the river was rising, but twenty were caught on a fly. The shooting party seemed quite happy about it, however, and I suspect they had had 'something' in their tea to keep the cold out during the long drive home with wet steaming dogs against their knees.

In low water quite a different technique is needed, and catching even a finnock is a real achievement. The river runs into a mere trickle, that one can cross dry-shod in shoes, between the still pools. With a bright sun on the water one has to stalk up the river bed and flick a dry-fly or a very small wet-fly gently on

The author's father with a day's catch of sea trout (40 lbs.) at Coruisk (Skye)

to the surface. It is only possible to hook one fish in a pool as the disturbance of playing it puts the rest down. The best pool for these methods is Stephen's pool, as a high tide just reaches it and it usually holds quite a few fresh and unsuspecting finnocks. The best time of day to try it is just before breakfast when the bacon is frying as one leaves the back door to go to the gunroom for a rod; and the best day is the first day of a holiday, whether as a small boy from school, or from the Air Force. After one has caught (or failed to catch) a fish one can walk along the bank and count every fish in the pool, which is quite shallow with every stone clearly visible, in low water.

Sea trout in a shallow pool resent being looked at and made to scurry up and down the pool; and after a while they retire beneath stones and sulk. If they have consistently refused to take a fly for several days and the water is shallow enough, there is a strong temptation to go in after them and remove them by hand. The noise they make as they feel one's hand and thump on the bottom of a stone always reminds me of the noise rabbits sometimes make when they are being bolted by ferrets!

Sometimes a larger fish is stranded in Stephen's pool: I remember two separate occasions, when I was a boy, finding a fish of eight pounds in the pool. They didn't last long, I am afraid. The first was extracted with a large triangle on a hand line, and the second with a garden fork. I was too young to be the culprit, but the question of leaving them was never even raised; I believe a lunch party on the following Sunday was used as an excuse by parents who had the poaching instinct well-developed, and have passed it on to their children.

On another occasion an enormous fish appeared in the Church pool, but here the problem wasn't so easy as the pool is very deep and there was a fair amount of water in the river at the time. The strawberry net was immediately taken from the bed and the strawberries left to the birds. We all liked strawberries but there was more important work for it. It was hurriedly converted into a fishing-net by the addition of weights to one end and floats to the other, and rushed up the river before the fish should make up its mind to set out for the loch.

Everybody turned out and my father directed operations. We managed to entangle the fish in the net once, and a great tail thrashed the surface for a moment, but a 12 lbs salmon is much stronger than a blackbird, and he broke the net, much to my father's disgust. The strawberries were covered with a terrific net next year. But enough of these poaching tricks, as I am sure they will be frowned upon by many people, although they should appeal to the man I once heard ordering a 'paternoster', in a famous London tackle shop, for use on a South-Country chalk stream. He said all the fish lived under the effluent of a flour mill and he intended fishing with that famous lure, 'Bakers' Glory.'

Dapping with a fly can be quite an effective way of catching sea trout in low water if there is a shoal under some trees and if one is prepared to keep very still for a long time. Even if they have been frightened they will settle down and a fish will eventually rise if one persists in bobbing a fly about over their heads. One year there was a large shoal in some comparatively deep water under the bank just above the stepping-stones near the mouth of the Kilmarie river. I used to spend hours on my tummy hidden by the long grass on the bank, dangling a fly on top of them. A fish would splash and take the fly from time to time, although each time a fish was hooked and landed the rest were put down.

I prefer a small rod about 8 ft long for fishing a little river, and I generally use a 2x point unless the river is very low, when a 3x point is better. A small bright fly is best for all occasions, the size varying slightly with the height of the water, and a 'Butcher' or a 'Bloody Butcher' is as good as any other for a river. The more I fish for sea trout the fewer are the patterns I use.

A fine evening is the time to catch fish from a dead-low river. Just when it is getting dark the fish take best, and it is advisable not to disturb the pool too early. Some friends who were sailing round the West Coast of Scotland in a very nasty little converted drifter, dropped in one evening, and when they had bathed and dined in comfort, David's thoughts turned to fishing. It was a lovely fine evening with the river dead low, so I took him to the Church pool just as it was getting dusk. I sat on top of the bank in the faint breeze and by smoking I managed to keep the midges at bay, but David was in the shelter of the bank and had some trouble with the clouds of midges which became entangled in the beard which life aboard his boat seemed to demand.

He fished and scratched for some time without success, but eventually the line tightened and he was fast in a fish which kept deep and played hard, out in the middle of the pool. I had no idea how large the fish was, but I thought it was probably about two pounds, and that it was taking a long time to play because he wasn't pulling at it hard enough. When it began to tire I scrambled down the rough rocks, crouched at the foot of the little waterfall and waited for him to bring the fish within the reach of the landing-net. It was very dark down below the high banks, with only a faint light reflecting from the broken water at the foot of the fall, and I couldn't see the fish unless it broke the surface. Eventually I saw a break in the blackness of calm water and netted where I thought the fish was, and raised the net. I was so surprised when I saw the fish that I nearly dropped it again, and I was very excited as I climbed back up the rocks to where David was standing. It was a lovely fresh sea trout and weighed 6 lbs, which is a big sea trout anywhere and the biggest to be caught from the Kilmarie river by fair means.

David and his crew came again to stay the following year; but this time the first night was cold and wet and the river was in a big spate. He suggested that we should go out again after dinner and he wouldn't believe a word of it when I told him it was no good. He went alone in the end. I only just refrained from saying 'I told you so', when he returned wet and empty-handed about an hour later and made for the whisky decanter.

Sea trout take a small minnow quite well in a spate and one can usually catch another two or three fish from a good pool after they have stopped taking a fly, but although they take with a bang and are fairly easily hooked it is surprising how many of the smaller fish get off when they begin jumping. I think the other hooks of a triangle often act as a fulcrum and the hook which has the hold is levered out of position by changes in the direction of strain. For this reason I much prefer fishing with a fly and seldom bother with a minnow, although it is sometimes fun to try a pool with a minnow after it has been fished with a fly. I have found that small gold and silver devons and phantoms are as good as any others when spinning in a river.

When I started fishing the Kilmarie river with a minnow I had no spinning reel or rod, so I used my ordinary reel and short fly-rod, pulling the line off the reel and holding a coil in my left hand, which I let go when I made the cast, and recovered to work the minnow. I spent one very wet morning fishing like this. The wind was from the South West blowing the wet Atlantic air from the sea, and the mist was low down on the hill. The burns appeared from below the swirling grey curtain as white streaks on the brown hillside. All the little streams that I crossed were full and hurried fussily to join the swirling current of the main river. I wasn't very clever at this method of fishing, as cold hands and wet bracken as high as one's waist on the banks of the pools made shooting the line very difficult. I only hooked and lost two little fish in the sheltered pools below the bridge. It was half-past twelve when I reached the Bridge pool and I was undecided whether to go home to lunch or fish another pool. I eventually decided to fish the Bend pool, which is the last pool below the loch, before lunch. It fishes best from the inside of the bend, with the bait working from the fast to the slacker water, but this would have meant a fairly long cast into the wind. As I was having difficulty in throwing the minnow more than a few yards I decided to try from the opposite bank with the wind behind me, and the strong current sweeping under the bank at my feet.

There was no shelter out on the open moor and the wind blew the rain in heavy squalls, flapping the macintosh about my wet legs. The wind was slightly up and across the stream and blew the rain in my face when I tried to fish downstream. My hands were soft and cold with the dripping wet and the line caught on buttons and bits of bracken as I tried to throw the minnow out across the wind, so my efforts weren't very successful. At last, just before going home to lunch I tried a final cast upstream from near the bottom of the pool. For once the line shot perfectly and the minnow landed with a little plop at the edge of the backwater on the far side of the strong current. I began to work it back towards me, but there was a big swirl almost as soon as it hit the water. I was fast in a good fish, with the slack line away and the strain running directly on to the reel. All went well as long as the fish was fresh and kept beyond the strong stream under my bank; but as soon as he began to tire, whichever way I pulled him was towards the strong water, and although I tried to pull him upstream, the current was too strong and eventually a very tired fish left the pool and went downstream, a dark grey shape in the swift broken water.

About sixty yards downstream there was a wood on my side of the river and a series of rocky falls down into the Church pool, an impossible place to follow a fish. The bank was fairly high and there was only one gap on it, about ten yards above the wood, where I could try to land the fish. It was a little backwater with a tuft of grass growing in the middle of it. I tried to get him above the tuft but he was just too strong and managed to get out into the current again. I knew that my last chance was below the tuft and I pulled as hard as I dared with a 2x gut trace. I just managed to work the fish into the slack water, and scoop him on to the bank with the small and rather rotten landing-net which I had with me. He was a grilse of 5 lbs with sea lice on him, but he didn't play as well as a sea trout of the same weight would have done, which was perhaps just as well or I should never have landed him.

CHAPTER XII

LOCH FISHING FOR SEA TROUT

I HAVE heard it said that loch fishing is dull compared with river fishing. This is about as true as it is to say that a fisherman must be very patient. Most fishermen are highly impatient people and loch fishing can never be dull if one approaches it from the right point of view. Some people think of a loch as a sheet of water, but to me it is a place of gravel rocks and weed, where fish do or don't lie, covered to varying depths with water. If one thinks of it like that it is just as exciting as a river.

A loch will fish well under far more varied conditions than a river, but it is much more difficult to forecast when fish will or won't take. This makes sea-trout fishing in lochs very fascinating although it can be exasperating at times. Are the fish going to take? In spite of hundreds of days on lochs which I have fished all my life, I still find this question impossible to answer with any degree of accuracy, as so often the best-looking days may be blank, and terrible days for fishing may prove to be terrific.

The usually accepted 'good fishing day' is one with a steady breeze to ripple the surface of the loch and drift the boat, and this incidentally makes casting very easy. Most people prefer a dull day, but I don't think it can be too bright unless the loch is very low and the temperature of the water high. I like a light 10-ft rod, and a good-sized reel as it is essential to have 100 yards of line and backing when fishing for sea trout.

If there is a breeze it is usually best to start fishing wet-fly, but even for this I always grease the line as it is much easier to strike a fish that takes at some distance from the boat if the line is on the surface. There is the disadvantage that sometimes sea trout will only take very deep, but this seldom happens and I always miss the ones that do take very deep, so it doesn't really

Head of Loch Coruisk (Skye)

matter. I like to throw a fairly long line and work the fly close to the boat by pulling the line in through the rings. One has to be careful how the coils of line fall in the boat and take care that it doesn't get caught round anything, if a fish takes and the line has to be let out in a hurry. The direction in which one casts depends on whether there is somebody else fishing in the boat or not. If one is alone the whole arc of water in front can be fished; but if there are two rods in the boat then only half must be fished.

I read one book which recommended the rods to fish out of the ends of the boat and work their flies parallel with the waves and not across them—just try it and see how long you keep your tempers! However hard one may try not to cast at the same time as the other rod, one is bound to do so sooner or later, and nothing is more infuriating than to be continually catching the other man's line behind the boat when both rods cast simultaneously. Whenever one wants to try a cast out of the end of the boat across wind, it is most important to wait until just after the other rod has cast.

It is well worth moving the fly through the water at varying speeds, as fish will take a slowly moving fly one day and only a fast-moving fly the next. After one has caught a few fish one knows more or less how the fish like the fly presented on that particular day. Most people fish with two or more flies, but at Strathaird we seldom use more than one although there are few weeds in the two biggest lochs, Na Creitach and Coruisk. We find that we catch just as many fish with one fly as when we try with two. A dropper is always a danger when playing a big fish, as it may become caught in the bottom in weeds, or in the net when the fish is being landed. I occasionally use two flies until I find what the fish are taking; but then I generally remove the dropper.

A floating fly is sometimes very effective even when there is a strong breeze and it is often the only thing a fish will take in a dead calm. But fish have an annoying way of rising to a floating fly with their mouths shut and trying to drown it, and one frequently foul hooks a fish on a floating fly. We generally use a claret and black or soldier palmer with plenty of hackle so that it sits well cocked up on the water. This is most important. I used to carry a bottle of oil to encourage the fly to float and one year I discovered some preparation that was supposed to have an irresistible smell for fish as well as making the fly float, but it was eventually discarded with many other fishing accessories. I now dry the fly by a slight flick behind, which can just be heard but isn't sufficient to flick off the fly—often!

Fish take a dry-fly in a number of different ways. Sometimes they just put their heads out, withdraw them again with the fly in their mouths—or they may make a head and tail rise, rolling over slowly like a porpoise. Occasionally there is a deafening splash which frightens one out of one's wits. One of the most exciting moments of any when sea-trout fishing is to see an enormous head appear where the small fly is floating, followed by a vast shoulder and dorsal fin and finally a wide black tail, and to see the line descend into the depths and feel it tighten in a large fish. On the whole more fish will be caught on a wet-fly than on a dry-fly; but my father used to fish with a dry-fly practically all the time for the best of all possible reasons, that he used to like seeing the fish's face come out of the water to take his fly. He was a great artist with a dry-fly for sea trout and if there was a ripple on the water he used to move the fly gently across the surface towards the boat. This slight animation often proved very effective.

It is sometimes difficult not to strike too soon and too hard, especially if one can see the fish coming up from a long way off, which is often possible, in the clear waters of Loch Coruisk, if the light is just right. Sometimes the light is good enough to see a fish at some distance from the boat and I am always surprised how brown they look in the water, but when they are coming at a fly one is usually aware of their white under-parts first, as the fish materialises just below the fly. I have never seen a fish coming from more than a few feet away but my father once saw one come right up from the bottom in about 30 ft of water; and I believe he took his fly away just as the fish arrived, he was so excited! This is only possible on a very calm day, but one often sees a fish appear in a wave on a bright day when there is a strong wind blowing, even when the fish never breaks the surface.

I have so often read that it is useless to fish on a dead-calm day, and yet I believe I have had more good days when it has been dead calm than under any other conditions. It is rather more difficult to cast and much more difficult to work the boat when there is no wind. The boat must be quietly rowed out from the shore and backed in again on a zig-zag in order to move down the loch over the lie of the fish. There must be no splashing and no rocking of the boat which will send great waves chasing each other across the calm surface. A very expert ghillie is needed to work a boat well on a calm day, and they are fairly rare, but with a good ghillie, a reasonable fisherman should have no difficulty in catching sea trout in a dead calm. It is best to start fishing with a floating fly, but if the fish won't look at it try a wet-fly as they will sometimes take a fly moving below the surface and refuse to look at one floating on top of it.

Imagine a brilliant sunny day in August without a breath of wind, the heat haze dancing over the rocks and heather and the sun's reflection from the water almost dazzling to the eyes. One day my mother and I arrived at Loch Na Creitach, a mile from Camasunary house, to find these conditions; the loch reflected the blue of the sky and the colours of the mountains like a sheet of glass except where an occasional catspaw of wind ruffled the surface. The water of the loch is absolutely clear and as the boat was pushed out into the deep water the reflections of the ripples it made danced across the green rocks many feet below until the water became too deep to see the bottom and the clear water became a translucent green.

According to the experts conditions were hopeless and we should have sat on the bank and admired the view or discussed politics, but we had an excellent boatman and it was well worth a try. We started fishing with floating flies cocked well up on the calm water, but although they looked very alluring the fish wouldn't look at them, so after an hour or so we tried sunk flies.

The day before had been Sunday and I had tied several flies

and among them a new pattern. I had a rather bad picture of a Peter Ross in a book which I had bought with prize money from Chemistry at school, and I tried to copy it. The fly I produced had golden pheasant tippet for a tail, a flat gold tinsel body, a scarlet hackle and a black hackle above it, and a teal wing, and this seemed an admirable opportunity to try it out. The fly looked very bright in the water, the scarlet hackle making the gold of the body very visible, and I could see the fly glinting in the water all the time I was working it towards the boat.

The fish took this fly very well, and when the light was right we could see them coming towards it for the last few yards and turn away with a flash of silver in the green water, and a swirl in the calm surface. It was very exciting as we rose a large number of fish. Most of the fish were about 1½ lbs, but I hooked a much larger one but unfortunately this broke me, as my line became caught round a button. This was a real tragedy as we only had two flies between us and this left us with only one. My mother went on fishing with it and I tried other flies in my box without success while she rose fish after fish, and eventually we took it in turns to use the 'gold fly' as it has been called ever since. We caught twenty sea trout that day averaging over a pound and had a wonderful thirst when it was time to go back to Camasunary house for tea.

Is there a more unlikely day than a dead calm with a bright sun? What about a dead calm with a steady downpour of rain and the mist a few hundred feet above the surface of the loch? I remember a day on Coruisk when the mist was motionless on the mountains and the black rocks were streaming with water. All the burns were breaking white down their rocky channels and the air was loud with the noise of many waters. It was fairly fine rain with the glassy calm surface of the loch pitted with millions of drops. We were soaked through within the first few hours and moved uncomfortably from side to side on the hard seats. We tried fishing with a dry fly, but it was hopeless trying to keep a fly on the surface as it became bedraggled and wet and sank in a few minutes; even while it was on the surface only a few wisps of feather remained above the water.

More in despair than hope I began fishing with a butcher. The fly fell into the water with a dull plop and after it had sunk a few inches I worked it towards the boat in little jerks. The fish came like demons and took with a great swirl, and for an hour or two we had such fun that we forgot our cold hands and wet clothes.

Too much wind is far worse for loch fishing than too little. Mr Peter Beckford says 'Take not out your hounds on a very windy day', and the same applies equally well to a fishing-rod. It is often too wild in Skye to get on to the lochs, but after several days of gale one may be tempted to try a loch against one's better judgement. The boat drifts much too fast and it is impossible to fish the water thoroughly. Rowing back for the next drift is very hard work and often takes nearly as long as the drift itself.

The actual fishing is anything but easy. If the cast is made in the ordinary way by moving the rod back and forward again in nearly the same plane, the fly usually ends up by wrapping itself firmly round the top of the rod. Even if the fly just touches the top of the rod without catching it, the chances are that on inspection one will find that a knot has been tied in the cast. I have never understood how these knots manage to tie themselves, but the less experienced the fisherman the more knots he manages to tie in his cast on a windy day. It is advisable to inspect the cast from time to time, as a plain knot is a point of weakness and a cast will always break there before anywhere else. The only way to avoid hitting the rod point with the fly is to make the rod point describe an ellipse during the cast. The stronger the wind the more nearly must the ellipse be to a circle. The fly then passes to the right of the rod on its way back, to the left on the way forward again.

When I am fishing in a high wind I always wear a hat, preferably a heavy sou'wester pulled well down over the back of my head, as I have no desire to wear sea trout flies as ear-rings until they can be sawn out by a doctor. Many's the time I have felt the fly whack the back of my head when I have been fishing a longer line than I should. It is a great mistake to try to cast too long a line in a high wind, but when the wind drops for a moment there is a temptation to lengthen the line. It is also definitely advisable to fish with only one fly. The cast can get into quite bad enough a tangle with one, and two make it all the worse. As with everything else there is a knack in undoing a raffle. The most important thing to remember is never to pull at it. Keep all the knots as loose as possible; a pin is useful for loosening knots, but I never have one with me and use the point of the hook. If a raffle won't yield to treatment in the first few minutes, take the fly or flies off and take the cast off the line; it is surprising how much easier it is to disentangle then and it only takes a second to tie the fly and cast on again. While undoing a raffle is one of the few occasions on which a fisherman has to have patience.

A friend of mine was coming to stay for the first time and I had told him he needed 60 yards of backing under the casting line on his reel. He had the silk backing on cardboard spools and he decided to put it on his reel during the train journey from Inverness to Kyle of Lochalsh. There were two old ladies on the opposite seat, knitting and reading. They watched with interest as he took the line off his reel and laid it on the seat and began to transfer the silk backing from the cardboard to his reel. But something went wrong; he probably tied the wrong end of the backing on to the centre of the reel, and very soon the whole thing was in the most terrible muddle. Eventually in desperation he began tugging at the knots. He went along to the dining-car for lunch, leaving the whole thing in a dreadful tangle on the seat. He spent a long time over lunch as he dreaded facing the tangle again; but he needn't have worried. When he returned, the line and backing were neatly coiled in two separate heaps on the seat and the two old ladies were back at their knitting.

The real trouble with a strong wind among high mountains is that it is always so gusty, especially if the wind direction isn't straight up the valley. One moment it may be quite calm and the swell has an oily look, while the next a black squall of wind comes tearing over the surface of the water and hits the boat with a bang. Sometimes it is quite impossible to cast again until the gust has died down. The gusts always seem to come when one has just reached a very likely place in the loch, with the result that the boat has passed the best place before one has a chance of fishing it properly.

Coruisk is much worse than Loch na Creitach for gusts. The loch is surrounded by a ring of mountains 3,000 feet high which rise very steeply from the loch. There is only one gap where the river runs out into Loch Scavaig. The wind comes through the gap in gusts and as it comes up the loch it is most impressive. One moment the boat may be rocking smoothly in the swell with only the sound of the wind high up among the rocks, where the grey mist is swirling, to break the stillness; then a squall of wind strikes the bottom of the loch and the black ruffles on the water, followed by angrily breaking waves, come roaring up. Sheets of spray are whirled into the air and the grass on the shores lies flat as the wind squall gets near the boat. In a second all is turmoil and noise, until the squall has passed and the air is quiet again except for the sound of the waves breaking on the rocky shore.

I have read somewhere that a big wave is an advantage when fishing for salmon in a loch, and I have on occasions caught a few large sea trout on a very windy day, but on the whole the lochs fish badly in a high wind. It is very difficult to keep a tight line when fishing on a rough loch as the line lying on the surface of the water is corrugated by the waves and this makes striking difficult. I believe sea trout are less accurate when they are rising to a fly on a rough day. Landing a big fish may be quite difficult, and it is best to get into a sheltered bay if possible.

I remember hooking a good sea trout at the head of Loch Coruisk during a calm spell on a windy day; but as soon as it was hooked a squall hit the boat. I had two men with me and they had to row as hard as they could into the wind to keep the boat in the same place, while I knelt in the middle of the boat to offer less resistance to the wind. The fish played well out from the boat, high in the water, and my line made an enormous bow from my rod point to the spot where it entered the water, which was most alarming. The wind roared on the water and hummed through the rings of my rod. I had to land the fish myself but I managed it, and it weighed 6 lbs; but the wind kept on blowing very hard, making it hopeless to go on fishing. We only just managed to row the boat back up the loch, gaining a few yards when the wind dropped a little and standing still or even losing a bit in the strong gusts.

On another occasion my brother was even less fortunate and had to leave the boat at the head of the loch and walk back. They pulled the boat well clear of the water and put some stones in the bottom of it, but not enough, for when they returned a few days later the boat had been lifted several yards by the wind and the bottom had been knocked out on a jagged rock.

The behaviour of sea trout in lochs is difficult to study and more difficult to explain: why will they lie and take in one place and not in another, and at one time of the day and not another? If I were to fish a strange loch with a ghillie who didn't know the water, I should start by rowing quietly round the whole loch with the fly trailing 40 yards behind the boat and remember where I had a pull or caught a fish. It is always a good plan to trail a fly while rowing upwind to start a drift. Sometimes fish will take a fly this way while refusing to look at one that is cast from a boat. Although it isn't such fun catching fish this way it is always fun catching fish, and it encourages the novice. Trailing is a useful way of finding what fly the fish will take on a particular day, especially at the beginning of a day, if the boat has to be rowed any distance before the first drift. One will start casting with a particular fly with much more confidence if it has already caught a fish.

Another way of finding where fish live is to watch the loch on a calm evening and see where they show. This isn't very reliable as fish often go together in shoals on a calm evening and move about the loch, but it gives quite a useful general idea of what part of the loch the fish live in.

Once fish have settled down in a loch I don't believe they move about a great deal, but this is impossible to prove. On Loch na Creitach the fishes' backs vary in colour, depending on the colour of the bottom on which they are lying. By looking at a fish it is often possible to tell which part of the loch it came from—but how long does it take for a fish's back to change colour? Probably only a day, so it doesn't really prove that fish stay in the same place. I have twice caught a fish in which a fly had been lost earlier in the day, and they were in exactly the same place; but the interval between losing the first fly and catching the fish was only a few hours, and although this supports my idea it doesn't prove it.

As a rule fish take best in from 15–50 feet of water where one can just see the bottom on a dull day, and it is well worth looking over the side of the boat from time to time to see what the bottom is made of and how deep the water is. Any place where there is a shallow patch well out from the shore, or where a ridge of rock or shingle runs out into the deeper water, is a likely spot for sea trout. For the first few days after they have left the sea fish are more apt to keep together in shoals than they are later in the season. This applies especially to Coruisk, as the journey from the sea is short and easy enough to enable the fish to swim up to the loch in a shoal.

After twenty years of fishing Loch na Creitach and Coruisk I know more or less where the fish live and take. Although the popularity of one spot may vary slightly from year to year, yet on the whole the successive generations of sea trout are remarkably conservative in their likes and dislikes. A stranger who went to fish either of these lochs, but especially Coruisk, would spend a tremendous amount of time fishing useless places. Loch Coruisk is 1½ miles long and except for the top 200 yards the whole of the West shore is useless. I don't know why this is —it looks just the same as the East shore, but although it has often been fished nothing but an occasional finnock has ever been caught from it, and no fish can be seen moving there on a calm evening. The East side has fish all the way along it, but there are two outstanding places—the shallows half-way up the loch and opposite the island where the terns nest, and the 'Rock' near the top. This is a low, smooth rock, about ten yards long and two wide, about eight yards from the shore. The ridge must run out for some distance under water and a tremendous number of fish live round it. It fishes best from the rock itself as one doesn't then disturb the water with the boat.

I remember one day in July when we had fished all the way to the Rock without rising a fish. As we drifted down on to it, I thought I saw a fish's head come out of the water and dip back again. Nobody else saw it, but when we reached the spot there was a swirl and I was fast in a fish. When he began to tire we could see he was a big fish and we watched every movement as he bored down into the clear green water.

The single strand of 2x gut seemed a very slender link between us. Eventually he tired and we netted him; he had sea lice on him and weighed 10 lbs, and he was the only fish we rose that day.

The top of the loch is quite shallow with a sandy bottom and fish seem to swim about over it rather than to rest there. In a high water they are near the top of the loch, but in a low water they tend to drop back into the slightly deeper water.

There is one small, fairly deep hole right at the top of the loch which must be scoured out by some current from the river which flows in there. It looks a dark purple on a dull day and is known as 'the black patch'. It can be most spectacular. Sometimes as soon as a fly lands over it there is a mighty swirl and one is fast in a fish weighing anything from 2–12 lbs. I have often caught half a dozen fish from it in rapid succession, keeping the boat well clear of the good place while the fish are being played.

I believe that in very deep lochs the secret is to find fish fairly near the surface and then they may take. On the bad days the fish are probably very deep, while on the good days they are in the shallower water or higher in the water. Most fish rise to a fly fairly soon after it has begun fishing and they rise without coming out of the water. This shows that they were near the fly and the surface before they decided to take; for if they came from a great depth and at any speed they would probably leave the water.

Fish probably spend a considerable time resting on the bottom and when they move about they will naturally be forced near the surface by shallow water; perhaps this is partly the reason why shallow ridges running out into the deep water fish so well. What determines the depth at which the fish swim? I don't know, as one can never tell beforehand when fish will or won't take on a loch. On two days which may seem identical to the fisherman sea trout may behave in completely different ways. The uncertainty is part of the fascination of loch fishing.

CHAPTER XIII

LOCH FISHING AT NIGHT

SEA trout in lochs do sometimes behave more regularly in the evening and at night than during the day; but before there is any chance of this the weather conditions must be just right. If the weather is fine for several days after a spate, the fish often behave in the same manner for a number of evenings, until the weather has been fine for some time and the water of the loch becomes very low and warm, when they sometimes go off completely. They also vary from year to year. I don't believe they have been taking so well at night recently as formerly, but this impression may be due to worse weather conditions in recent years. Sea trout sometimes take well on a windy evening, but they go off as it begins to get dark unless the wind drops to a gentle breeze.

During very fine weather the wind is generally southerly, blowing in from the sea during the day. As the land becomes warmer than the sea in the hot sun, the air in contact with it is heated and rises, and cool air flows in from the sea. At night the reverse takes place. As the sun gets low and the rocks and heather of the mountains begin to cool, the sea breeze drops and the lochs become calm. Later on after the sun has set, a gentle breeze often springs up from the North. It is better for fishing if the wind stays in the South, as the glow from the sunset remains in the Northern sky for a long time after the rest of the sky is the deep blue of the night. The reflection of the light on the water makes it possible to see a rise much later than if the wind is from the North when one is fishing into the darkness.

The best night's fishing there has ever been at Strathaird was at the beginning of July, but it is quite possible to have a bad or even a blank night when fishing in July. The first fortnight in August is probably the best for night fishing. There is a long twilight from about 10 p.m. until after midnight, and most of

Loch na Creitach (Skye)

the big fish are up, with a sufficient number of smaller ones to keep one amused if the big ones won't play the game.

The moon seems to make little difference to night fishing. The fish generally stop rising when all trace of daylight has left the sky and the moon has little effect on the time the fish go off the rise, but it can make it easier to see a rise if one is fishing into the streak of light where it is reflected from the water.

The loch is in shadow by about 8 o'clock as the sun sinks behind the high ridge of the Cuillins to the West. As the wind drops the water becomes a glassy calm, broken only by the rings from rising fish. About this time the fish often come to the surface in shoals and move about the loch just dimpling the surface from time to time. For a while they behave in the same way they used to behave when they were in the sea waiting to run up to the lochs, and they often move right out over the deep water near the centre of the loch.

They aren't easy to catch as they always seem to be rising everywhere except within reach of the boat, and the water is so calm that it is difficult to manoeuvre the boat within reach of a shoal without sending out little waves which make the fish move further away. A dry fly is the best chance of rising these cruising fish, but they won't always take even if the fly lands right among them. Often there is only a little dimple to show that a fish has come right up to the fly to look at it; but sometimes the fish take quite well. Once a fish is hooked in deep water its main object seems to be to go as deep as possible. I have often had a large fish go almost straight down for 40 yards in the first rush.

When the last rays of sunshine leave the peaks and it begins to get dark the fish move inshore. When it is too dark to see a rise they are often in only a few feet of water and quite often take a fly very well indeed.

I first noticed at a very early age that the inside rod at night caught most fish even when there was a strong wind. I was fishing Loch na Creitach one evening with my father, and the boat had to be kept with the bows out as there was quite a strong wind, so it was easier to work the boat this way. He rose fish after fish while I never moved a thing, and although he was much the better fisherman, I should at least have risen an odd fish. This made me think that perhaps the fish were lying close in and I have proved it many times on Loch na Creitach since then.

A few nights later we were fishing the top end of Loch na Creitach and the ghillie had the boat well out over a shallow where the fish sometimes take well during the day. We did no good, so, as I suggested, we went right in close. I was inside rod and I began catching fish at once. I caught four while my father never had a rise, but he was still very sceptical about my theory that the inside rod had much the best chance. However, I eventually insisted on turning the boat round so that he was fishing nearest the shore. It was getting very dark and we drifted for some distance without anything happening.

Eventually my father said: 'Well I don't think much of this, hullo what's happened?' He was fast in a fish which tore out from the shallow into the deep black water of the loch and played very hard and deep down. It is difficult to land a fish at night as one can only see where the fish is when it breaks the water and sends out ripples. We only had a small net; but the ghillie managed to get the fish into it, and although there was an ominous crack from the shaft of the landing-net as he lifted the fish aboard, it was safely in the boat. It weighed 11 lbs when we got it home.

During the early part of the evening a fairly fine cast is best especially if it is very calm, but later on when the light begins to go it is advisable to fish with a much heavier cast, either strong sea trout or light grilse. When it begins to get really dark the thickness of the cast makes no difference to the fish taking. A thick cast makes it possible to play and land a fish much more quickly, which is most important when the rise may last for only half an hour. It is maddening to have to wait ten minutes while a 2-lb sea trout is being played, when fishing time is so precious.

On a fine night a large number of heather moths come fluttering out of the grass and heather, and fly out over the loch. The fish which move close inshore are waiting for the ones that go solo too soon and crash in the first few yards. Any fly will do as it is seen by the fish as a dark silhouette against the sky, and I don't believe fish can see colours at night any more than we can. The fly that we have found best for fishing at night was invented by my brother Maurice. I tie large numbers of them every year. I shall be out of a job after the war as the Germans have got him shut up too and he is learning to tie his own flies. It is a simple fly consisting of three fibres of red hackle for the tail, a grey wool body with silver tinsel, a red hackle, and a white wing, made from any seagull feather; but a teal and silver is nearly as good.

On a calm night it soon becomes too dark to see a rise, especially if one is fishing from a boat towards a steep shore. The reflection is often so perfect that one can't see where the water ends and the land begins. When it grows too dark to see where the fly is falling, the length of line out has to be measured by the feel of the weight of the line that one is casting. This sounds difficult; but it soon becomes quite easy and I am sure that a blind man could soon learn to cast very expertly by the feel alone; and what a good night fisherman he would make! If the weight or the sound of the line seems wrong during a cast it is a good plan to reel in and feel along the cast to make sure there isn't a raffle. If there is a bad raffle and you have no torch it is probably time to go home.

When it becomes too dark to see a rise the striking has to be done entirely by feel. It is most essential to have the line well greased so that any touch on the fly can be felt at once, as sea trout take in quite a different way at night. All that is felt is a very gentle draw on the fly; but if one delays the strike for a second, thinking that such a gentle touch can't possibly be a fish, it is too late. A heavy weight is felt for only a second when one does eventually decide to strike. As soon as the slightest touch is felt or even imagined, that is the time to strike, quick and hard. The very quickness of the strike makes one strike much too hard for a normal 2x cast, and for this reason also it is essential to have a stronger cast. If the fish is under 2 lbs it will probably be thrashing on the surface a second after the strike, but the excitement begins when there is an unresponsive weight like a log out in the dark water close under the bank, firmly attached to the fly. It doesn't stay still for long, as a big fish races for deep water the moment it is hooked, the line tearing through the darkness. A large net is most useful at night. We now use a salmon net, which enables one to land a fish more quickly and avoids the risk of missing and frightening a fish which is difficult to see. Very often the first idea one has of the size of a fish one has been playing is when it is lifted into the boat, a pale silver shape in the dark net.

It is the usual custom for one rod to stop fishing while the other is playing a fish. This is a good plan if the fish is of any size; but if it is less than 2 lbs it is hardly necessary. The rod who isn't playing the fish must take care not to interfere with the one who is playing the fish, and he should avoid doing what I did one night. My brother Mark was playing quite a small fish and I went on fishing out of the end of the boat to keep my line well clear of his. I rose a fish and struck and felt the fish just hard enough to bend my rod double before he came off. My line flew back and there was a howl of surprise and anguish as the fly impinged upon Mark's ear with no little force. Luckily the flat of the fly and not the point hit him and it didn't even cut his ear, but apparently it hurt quite a lot. It would have made an awful mess of it had it hit him point first.

The fish behave much more regularly on Loch na Creitach than on Loch Coruisk. On a good night one should catch from 10 to 15 fish weighing from 1 to 12 lbs, but I have often had over 20. The majority of big fish weighing over 8 lbs are caught at night. Soon after Maurice had designed his fly he caught a beautiful fish of 10 lbs on it one night on Loch na Creitach. We went back over the hill next morning as his leave was up and he had to rejoin his regiment. Before driving him to the ferry I made a quick outline-drawing on a sheet of newspaper of the fish, which he took with him, as we were decorating the walls of Camasunary with drawings of fish weighing over 8 lbs. I returned to find an over-zealous domestic had 'cleaned up' the sheet of paper.

I had to make the drawing from memory and I wanted to do

the fish full justice. Unfortunately I was over enthusiastic and although I carved a bit off its stomach every year with a pair of scissors it is still much too fat.

Coruisk is never so certain at night as Loch na Creitach. Here it is much more important that the weather should be really fine; but it can fish wonderfully well at times. If there is any chance of it being a wild night it isn't worth while going there, quite apart from the difficulty of getting back the two miles of open sea in a small boat on a rough dark night.

On a fine night it is the most wonderful place on earth. As the light begins to fade out and the colours go, the mountains merge with their reflections. The black shadows of night spread from the mountains across the glassy calm of the loch. The pale glow of the Northern sky reflected from the centre of the loch is the only pool of light amid the darkness. It is the hour when the little men come out from the great cairns of rocks and the water horse emerges from its cave in the mountain and swims in the clear water. When Peter MacIntyre was a young man, the party he was rowing on Loch na Creitach one dark night was driven from the loch by a strange unearthly cry. After it had been repeated twice, the 'gentleman' said: 'If I hear that again I am going home.' They heard it and went. Peter was quite glad to go, as who can tell what is abroad in those old dark mountains? But on thinking it over afterwards, he decided that the sound was probably made by a fox.

Maurice was fishing Coruisk one night with a friend. When they were half-way up the loch they heard the terns, which had long since gone to roost, begin to stir; and very soon every tern was in the air, filling the night with cries of danger. They looked around and emerging from the dark shadow of the mountain they saw a disturbance in the water: pale shimmering waves spread out across the still loch behind a black object which moved steadily through the water. It was just at the time of the Loch Ness Monster and I believe they debated upon rowing rapidly for the shore, until the object came into the clear reflection of the sky and they saw it was the head of a red deer hind making straight for the tern island. The terns went on making a terrible commotion until the boat was out of hearing.

A few days before, we had landed on the tern island to look for nests and baby terns, and we were surprised to find a large number of dead babies with their heads missing. We thought at the time that a fox must have swum across and killed them; but the day after we saw the hind we again visited the island and found a fresh batch of decapitated corpses with their blood newly dried on their fluffy grey feathers. This and the fuss that the terns made seemed to prove that a hind was the culprit. Lachy Robertson who lives at Camasunary told me a story which tended to confirm this. He had some snares set within twenty yards of his cottage one winter, and one morning he heard a rabbit squealing like mad; he looked out and saw a hind standing over the rabbit. The squealing stopped as he ran outside and the hind galloped away when she saw him appear; but in the snare was the body of a rabbit still bleeding and with no head. The Cuillins are of igneous rock and there is no calcium in the water that runs from them. In South Africa cattle suffer from 'Pica', or depraved appetite, and chew the bones of dead animals. It is known that deer eat shed antlers, and perhaps this hind was feeding a calf which made a heavy demand on the calcium in her blood and drove her to eat the skulls of terns to supply this demand.

Since the fish move right inshore at night it seems logical to fish for them from the bank. I have had some good evenings doing so, but there are two disadvantages. The first is that the midges are never quite so fierce out on the loch as they are on the shore, and they can make life a misery if one tries to fish from the bank. The other is the difficulty of moving along the bank. It is easy enough if there is a shingle beach, but most of the shore of Coruisk is great boulders piled haphazard on top of one another and jutting out into the loch. They are difficult enough to walk over during the day, and at night it is almost impossible without the danger of falling and breaking a rod. On the whole one is much better off fishing from a boat than from the bank. I have had one good evening fishing from the bank on Coruisk when there were two other people to fish from a boat; but I chose a fairly level stretch of shore where a burn runs into the loch. I caught 13 sea trout, but they were mostly under 1 lb. The men fishing the boat didn't catch quite so many, but they had some good fish, the biggest weighing 7 lbs.

When the fish decide to take on Coruisk at night they sometimes surpass themselves. They keep together in shoals to a much greater extent than they do in Loch na Creitach, and they aren't so keen to move close inshore when it gets dark. I fished Coruisk two nights running, once, with my mother. The weather was perfect and each night just as it was getting very dark an enormous shoal of fish began dimpling the surface near the rock. The first night they were in the little bay just to the south of the rock, and the next night they were about 200 yards off directly opposite the rock. As soon as a fly landed near them a fish took and we had about an hour's wonderful sport on both occasions until they decided to go off the rise. The best night ever was had on Coruisk by Mark and Aylmer in the middle of July. It never gets quite dark in July and they fished all through the night until it began to get light. The fish rose the whole time and were still rising when they stopped fishing, but they were too tired to go on. The small fish weren't up but all the larger ones were, and they caught 15 sea trout weighing 73 lbs. Five weighed over 8 lbs; the biggest was 9 lbs, and they hooked and broke in several other whales.

The biggest sea trout we have ever caught at Strathaird was in Coruisk, and weighed 13½ lbs. It was caught by day trailing a salmon fly, but I am sure a bigger one will be caught one day on a cast fly at night. I believe I hooked him the last night's fishing I had there. It was towards the end of July 1940 when I was waiting to join the R.A.F. and train as a pilot. It was a perfect night with a gentle breeze from the South and I was fishing at the top end of the loch. There were three fish in the boat weighing 2 lbs, 3 lbs, and 6 lbs, which were caught in quick succession from the black 'patch' just as it was getting dark. Then for some time nothing moved. The boat was close inshore near some enormous boulders which had fallen from the steep bank into the loch during some bygone age. The water was about 15 ft deep and the bottom sandy. I felt a slight draw on the line, struck, and felt the heavy solid weight of a large fish. He went off with the reel screaming, and when he was about 30 yards from the boat he jumped several feet in the air. The moon had risen over the mountains and threw a ray of silver on the rippling surface. I could just see the fish in the faint light, and put him down as about 15 lbs. I had a new strong cast and a fairly large fly so there seemed a fine chance of landing him. He jumped again rather closer to the boat and we confirmed his size; but a moment later the line went slack with only the drag of the water against it as I reeled sadly in, and the biggest sea trout I have ever hooked sank back into the deep, dark waters of the loch. Maybe one day I shall catch a monster yet.

The sea trip from Scavaig back to Camasunary is wonderful on a calm night. The smell of the sea hangs on the cool air, and the phosphorescent wake from the outboard motor stretches back a pale streak in the darkness towards the black mountains. The boat rises and falls on the gentle swell, making its way out to sea to round the headland of Sgurr na Strie. Once round the last point Camasunary house comes into sight and an orange glow in the window shows that the party from Loch na Creitach is already back. As they sit in the warm sitting-room in front of a peat fire they can hear the outboard motor as soon as the boat rounds the point and heads for the river mouth, and put a kettle on the primus to boil. The door opens and everyone goes into the kitchen where the fish are emptied into the sink, a slither of silver in the flickering candle light. Notes are compared over a steaming cup of cocoa and then to bed, often as dawn begins to break, a cold grey light over heather rock and water.

Mouth of Coruisk River (Skye)

CHAPTER XIV

ABOUT SEA TROUT

THERE is a particular fascination in fishing for migratory fish; they are so completely wild. When one catches a brown trout there is the feeling that there is one less fish in the water, and if one catches a large and well-known trout from a small stream it is almost like losing an old friend when one says 'good-bye' to him. With migratory fish there is no such feeling. They are only passing through, and the other dangers they have to face are so much greater than that of being caught on a rod, that one need have little compunction in catching as many as possible; whereas all but the most subdued consciences are apt to stir if one takes a large basket of brown trout from a heavily fished stream.

There is more uncertainty and luck in catching migratory fish, for besides the question whether they will take, there is often a doubt whether they will be there at all. It makes a good day all the more enjoyable. I always feel a strange excitement when I see a large shoal of fresh fish jumping in the bay, waiting for a spate to run up into the rivers and lochs.

How do fish return year after year to the same rivers and lochs? We pass it off easily as 'instinct'; but what a tremendous amount is concentrated in that word, and what a wonderful memory a fish must have for the feel of currents and temperatures to be able to return to the river where it was hatched.

Everybody who catches sea trout or salmon must want to know something of their life history and habits. There are many good books on the subject and for sea trout there is none better than *The Life of The Sea Trout* by G. H. Nall. I have a copy to which I am continually referring. The sea trout or Salmo Trutta is anatomically indistinguishable from the brown trout. It differs only in its habits, for it migrates to the sea after two or three or four years in fresh water. Unlike the salmon, however, it returns to fresh water every year for a few months, even before it is sexually mature, for it may not spawn before its third or fourth return. On its first return, when it corresponds to the salmon grilse, it weighs about $\frac{3}{4}$ lb and is known by many local names, such as 'herling' or 'finnock'. It is undoubtedly a very stupid little fish and it will take practically anything when it first comes into the river. I was fishing the fisherman's pool at Camasunary one day with a cast which had a red loop. I rose a number of fish without hooking any, until I actually saw a fish come and bite the loop of the cast where it was attached to the line. It is great fun catching a large number of fish in a short time as it happens so seldom; but it is a mistake to keep more finnocks than one needs for eating, as every larger fish has to pass through the finnock stage.

As no two rivers are exactly the same, the sea trout vary widely in their habits from one river to another. If one visits the same place for a number of years it makes the fishing far more interesting if one knows something of the life history of the fish one catches. The only way to do this is to read the scales of the fish. This sounds fearfully scientific and few people try it; but anyone can discover a certain amount without any difficulty. Only a very low-powered microscope is needed—the sort one gives to a child on his twelfth birthday, and there are many books which explain how to read scales, with photographs and diagrams which illustrate the text admirably. When one examines a natural scale the picture isn't always as clear as the book would have one believe, but one can always learn something from it.

A fish's scale looks rather like the cross section of a tree split in two. Rings are added at regular intervals, and they are close together when the fish is growing slowly and wide apart when it is growing rapidly. It is quite easy to see where it first migrated to the sea as there are wide bands surrounding the narrow bands in the centre, which represent the parr years before it migrated; but I found great difficulty in telling the number of parr years it had spent before migrating. Once a sea trout has migrated, it returns to the river every summer and back to the sea in the Autumn. It is quite easy to tell the difference between the quick growth in the sea and the very slow growth in the fresh water and to count the number of times it has returned. When a sea trout spawns it loses much condition before it reaches the sea again, and there is an absorption of material from the edges of the scales where they fit into the sac in the skin. This is made good when it begins feeding again, but the lines at the edge of the scale are broken. This is known as the 'Spawning Mark'. It can be easily seen if there has been much loss in condition, but not so easily if the loss in condition was only slight. An amateur may have difficulty in reading the parr years and spawning marks correctly, but nobody could go wrong over the number of times the fish has migrated and this in itself is sufficiently interesting to make the study worth while. I have managed to interest quite a few people in it, and I am sure that if people realised how simple it is, more would read the scales of the salmon and sea trout that they catch.

For several years I collected the scales of the largest fish we caught at Strathaird, and practised reading them through a microscope that had been given to my brother when he was young. One year I decided to do it more thoroughly. I examined every sea trout that we caught that summer, about 700 in all. It was very amateurish as we did no netting, but I found out some very interesting facts about the sea trout from the three different river systems at Strathaird; the Kilmarie river, the Camasunary river and lochs, and Coruisk.

I weighed and measured the length and girth of every fish, and took a few scales each night, when the fish were brought in from the various lochs. It was often rather a rush as the parties might not be back until half-past seven and dinner was supposed to be at eight. With twenty or thirty fish to weigh and measure before having a bath, I was often late for dinner; but if they were left an over-zealous kitchen-maid had usually desecrated the bodies before I could deal with them. I used to put the weights and measures on little bits of paper and wrap the scales up in them until the morning, when I read the scales through the microscope and entered my sometimes doubtful conclusions in a large notebook with a separate place for each river system.

I didn't examine enough fish from the little river and loch at Kilmarie to be able to form an accurate picture of the average rate of growth of the fish; but the comparison between Camasunary and Coruisk was interesting. The spawning beds at Camasunary are in the burns that run into Loch an Athain, and most fish spawn in the Fruach Corry burn a mile or so above the loch. To reach this burn they have to swim 1½ miles from the sea to Loch na Creitach and jump some considerable falls; 1 mile through Loch na Creitach and 1 mile on to Loch an Athain, which is almost a ¼ mile square; not very far but twice the distance they have to go to Coruisk. Loch Coruisk is 1½ miles long, but it is only a few hundred yards from the sea and at high tide the fish can swim straight into the loch without meeting any fall. The spawning beds are in the burn running into the head of the loch from Corry Uisge, and the furthest the fish can go is ¾ mile from the loch where the water comes sheer down the rough black rocks of the Cuillins. The waters of both river systems are absolutely clear, with no stain of peat, as there are no peat beds and the water comes straight from hard igneous rock, gabbro and granite, of the Cuillins. The mouths of the two rivers are about two miles apart, and the fish come into them at the same time of the year; the larger fish at the end of June and in July, and the smaller ones through August and September.

There is very little feed in either Coruisk or the Camasunary lochs but possibly a little more at Camasunary. A fresh-water biologist once came and trailed little nets about Coruisk all day. To the delight of the ghillies who were rowing him, and to his disgust he found nothing at all, but there must be some feed or the parr would not be able to grow large enough to migrate to the sea. It is generally accepted that salmon do not feed in fresh water and that sea trout do. This is true, but sea trout needn't feed in fresh water because there isn't enough food at Coruisk to support the number of fish that it holds, and yet the rate of growth at Coruisk is greater than that of Camasunary fish. They are both greater than the growth rate of the Kilmarie

A Bavarian stream

The author and his brother Maurice; first day back for Two ex-P.O.W.

river fish where there is food. The average weight of sea trout on their second return from the sea is 1.0 lb at Kilmarie, 1.2 lbs at Camasunary, and 1.6 lbs at Coruisk. On their third return it is 2.0 lbs at Camasunary and 2.7 lbs at Coruisk.

Another point is that the spawning marks on the Coruisk fish are always faint and sometimes almost impossible to see, whereas the Camasunary fish generally have fairly distinct spawning marks. The explanation of all this is that the Coruisk fish lose less condition in reaching the spawning beds and return to the sea more easily and rapidly after spawning, where they immediately continue feeding and put on weight.

Brown trout in the local burns never get bigger than about a quarter of a pound and are always in bad condition. The amount of food that a large sea trout could pick up would not be worth the energy, and the less time he spends in the fresh water the faster he grows and the larger he becomes.

I also cleared up another point, to my own satisfaction anyway! I had noticed previously that one was apt to underestimate the weight of a fish caught at the beginning of the season and overestimate the weight at the end of the season. I found the explanation for this by consulting the weights and measurements of fish caught in July and comparing them with the figures for September.

I write this with some trepidation for I have never seen it mentioned anywhere before. I had the measurements of the length, girth and weights of all the fish, and I found that if a fish of certain measurements weighed 6 lbs at the beginning of the season, another fish of exactly the same measurements would only weigh 5¾ lbs two months later. The probable explanation is that the development of the sexual organs and the call on the hard firm muscles of the body, lowers the density of the fish. The muscle doesn't diminish much in volume; but energy is continually being used up and the muscle becomes less dense as the season progresses, and weighs less for the same volume. This tendency would be natural even if the fish were maintaining its condition, for salt water is denser than fresh water and a fish leaving salt water for fresh water should become slightly less dense to allow for this, and enable its swim bladder, which deals with slight changes in density, to act normally.

A most important problem for the fisherman is why do salmon and sea trout take in fresh water when they do not have to eat in order to live? There are various reasons put forward, anger, curiosity, memories of parr-hood days, when they fed in fresh water, and many others. They may all be true but there is another which I am convinced is responsible for fish taking. There is a strongly developed instinct in all animals to kill anything that is weak or ill. If a terrier gets into a trap other terriers will immediately set on him, and if two hounds are fighting in kennel, the rest of the pack will attack and kill the first hound that is injured. The same applies to fish, and that is partly the reason why a streak of red in a fly or on a bait is so often deadly.

I first discovered this when I was trailing a fly on Loch an Athain one day. I felt a little fish take the fly and I hoped he would get off; but he didn't, so I pulled the rod point forward and then let the line slack, hoping that it would dislodge him. When I tightened again there was a heavy weight on the line and I imagined that the little fish had come off and the fly had been taken by a larger one. The fish played deep and sullenly with a heavy log-like strain, and he only came to the surface once, some yards from the boat, when I saw that he was a sea trout of 6 lbs or so. A few minutes later he came off and I reeled in to find a much mangled parr still attached to the hook. This also accounted for the sullen way in which the sea trout played: a direct pull on his lunch wasn't calculated to make him play in a very lively manner! Curiously enough exactly the same thing happened to my brother Mark on Loch na Creitach the same year.

We don't use minnows at Strathaird and we were quite properly forbidden to do so as children, but a small fish mounted on a spinning tackle is very deadly. When the fish wouldn't look at a fly we were occasionally tempted, and I remember the code name for the performance was a 'teal and green' so that the family should not discover that we had been using a minnow!

Also available from Excellent Press

A GAMEKEEPER'S NOTEBOOK
Jones and Woodward
ISBN 1 900318 1 64
£18.95

THE GAMEKEEPER AT HOME
Richard Jefferies
ISBN 1 900318 20 2
£18.95

THE AMATEUR POACHER
Richard Jefferies
ISBN 1 900318 22 9
£18.95

WHERE THE BRIGHT WATERS MEET
Harry Plunkett Green
ISBN 1 900318 21 0
£19.95

COUNTRYMAN'S COOKING
W,M.W. Fowler
ISBN 1 900318 29 6
£16.95

EXCELLENT PRESS
9 Lower Raven Lane, Ludlow, Shropshire SY8 1BW
Tel: 01584 877803 · Email:excellent.press@ukonline.co.uk